Bleeding Kansas

by Kathryn Walat

A Samuel French Acting Edition

New York Hollywood London Toronto

SAMUELFRENCH.COM

Copyright © 2011 by Kathryn Walat
ALL RIGHTS RESERVED

CAUTION: Professionals and amateurs are hereby warned that *BLEEDING KANSAS* is subject to a Licensing Fee. It is fully protected under the copyright laws of the United States of America, the British Commonwealth, including Canada, and all other countries of the Copyright Union. All rights, including professional, amateur, motion picture, recitation, lecturing, public reading, radio broadcasting, television and the rights of translation into foreign languages are strictly reserved. In its present form the play is dedicated to the reading public only.

The amateur and professional live stage performance rights to *BLEEDING KANSAS* are controlled exclusively by Samuel French, Inc., and licensing arrangements and performance licenses must be secured well in advance of presentation. PLEASE NOTE that amateur Licensing Fees are set upon application in accordance with your producing circumstances. When applying for a licensing quotation and a performance license please give us the number of performances intended, dates of production, your seating capacity and admission fee. Licensing Fees are payable one week before the opening performance of the play to Samuel French, Inc., at 45 W. 25th Street, New York, NY 10010.

Licensing Fee of the required amount must be paid whether the play is presented for charity or gain and whether or not admission is charged.

Professional/stock licensing fees quoted upon application to Samuel French, Inc.

For all other rights than those stipulated above, apply to: The Gersh Agency, 41 Madison Avenue, New York, NY 10010; attn: Seth Glewen.

Particular emphasis is laid on the question of amateur or professional readings, permission and terms for which must be secured in writing from Samuel French, Inc.

Copying from this book in whole or in part is strictly forbidden by law, and the right of performance is not transferable.

Whenever the play is produced the following notice must appear on all programs, printing and advertising for the play: "Produced by special arrangement with Samuel French, Inc."

Due authorship credit must be given on all programs, printing and advertising for the play.

ISBN 978-0-573-69915-3   Printed in U.S.A.   #29802

No one shall commit or authorize any act or omission by which the copyright of, or the right to copyright, this play may be impaired.

No one shall make any changes in this play for the purpose of production.

Publication of this play does not imply availability for performance. Both amateurs and professionals considering a production are strongly advised in their own interests to apply to Samuel French, Inc., for written permission before starting rehearsals, advertising, or booking a theatre.

No part of this book may be reproduced, stored in a retrieval system, or transmitted in any form, by any means, now known or yet to be invented, including mechanical, electronic, photocopying, recording, videotaping, or otherwise, without the prior written permission of the publisher.

MUSIC USE NOTE

Licensees are solely responsible for obtaining formal written permission from copyright owners to use copyrighted music in the performance of this play and are strongly cautioned to do so. If no such permission is obtained by the licensee, then the licensee must use only original music that the licensee owns and controls. Licensees are solely responsible and liable for all music clearances and shall indemnify the copyright owners of the play and their licensing agent, Samuel French, Inc., against any costs, expenses, losses and liabilities arising from the use of music by licensees.

IMPORTANT BILLING AND CREDIT REQUIREMENTS

All producers of *BLEEDING KANSAS* must give credit to the Author of the Play in all programs distributed in connection with performances of the Play, and in all instances in which the title of the Play appears for the purposes of advertising, publicizing or otherwise exploiting the Play and/or a production. The name of the Author *must* appear on a separate line on which no other name appears, immediately following the title and *must* appear in size of type not less than fifty percent of the size of the title type.

In addition the following credit *must* be given in all programs and publicity information distributed in association with this piece:

Bleeding Kansas **was first produced as a world premiere by**
The Hangar Theatre
(Kevin Moriarty, Artistic Director; Lisa Bushlow, Executive Director)
in Ithaca, New York in August 2007.

CHARACTERS

HANNAH ROSE ALLEN – A young abolitionist from Boston.

EDWIN REDPATH aka **RED** – A pro-slavery "Border Ruffian" from Missouri.

KITTSON CLARKE – A headstrong woman following her husband George.

GEORGE CLARKE – A free-state farmer from Indiana.

JOSIAH NICHOLS – A pro-slavery farmer from Missouri.

OTHER MEN – Played by the actors who play Red, George, and Josiah, as indicated.

SETTING

Kansas Territory

TIME

1855-1856

AUTHOR'S NOTES

This play is set in a historical time and place. But then, history is happening all around us.

HISTORICAL NOTE

In 1854 the Kansas-Nebraska Act established the territories of Kansas and Nebraska, opening the land to legal settlement. It also stipulated that the residents of these territories would decide by popular vote if their state would enter the Union as a "free" or "slave" state – a concept of self-determination known as popular sovereignty.

People on all sides of this hotly contested issue flooded the territory, in an attempt to sway the vote in their favor. Three distinct political groups occupied Kansas: pro-slavers (many from neighboring slave state Missouri), free-staters (farmers looking to better their lot in the territory), and abolitionists (a small but vocal group mostly from New England).

While many free-state Kansans seemed to care little about slaves, and many pro-slavery Kansans never owned a single slave, violence broke out almost immediately between these opposing factions, largely fueled by election fraud, rival territorial governments, and squabbles over land claims. After reaching its peak during the bloody summer of 1856, the violence continued until 1861, when Kansas entered the Union as a free state.

This era – during which the territory became one of the first battlegrounds over the question of slavery – is now known as "Bleeding Kansas." It is a snapshot of a country, politically divided and ready to shed blood over issues of God and man.

ACT I

Scene One: This Here's Kansas Territory

(From the darkness of the stage, we hear sounds of freedom and anticipation mixed with danger riding across the land. This is Kansas territory, the new frontier, a rough and wild place to be. In the morning sunlight, we see **HANNAH ROSE ALLEN***, a young Boston abolitionist. She is inside a letter.)*

HANNAH. *America.* Dear Abigail, that's what I thought. Looking out the back flap of the wagon. This is America. No, even better: America's *future.* You should have seen it, Abby – as far as the eye can reach, nothing but a beautiful green carpet, save here and there a cluster of trees. And I felt nothing but awe in view of this infinite display.

Until I pricked my finger on the sewing needle – yes, because I didn't *secure* my needle before wondering at the glory of America – and sucking on my bloody finger, I tasted yesterday's salted dinner and the fire that warmed it and the horses I fed this morning, together with the rich frontier soil – and I thought heck, and just threw that sampler overboard, dear sister, because this place is nothing like Boston.

This is Kansas. Three parts danger, one part home.

(We see the rough and almost-clean frontier cabin of the Clarkes. **KITTSON CLARKE** *stands out front, looking at their farm, which is modest but theirs. Shielding the Kansas wind with her cupped hands, she lights a corncob pipe.)*

KITTY. Dear George. So. This is *Kansas*. Not that I've complained. Since we set foot here and I found our temporary shelter would be a *lean-to*. Open on *two* sides, so that Kansas wind could blow right through – made powerful sense when I washed my one pair of bloomers, dried them quicker than you could say: My, *Kansas*…

So I didn't say nothing, George, about the cookin' out of doors, stamping on the bottom of my skirt when it catch fire. Enjoyed that *red* complexion the open flame gave me. Could throw an Indian blanket over my head, pass myself for a *squaw*.

*(We see **EDWIN REDPATH**. You can call him **RED**. A young man, but still, he's been drinking bad whiskey for almost a decade now. He has long boots, covered in dust and mud. Unshaven face. Unwashed hands. He spits. Looks around. He's looking for trouble. He's a Border Ruffian.)*

RED. Chicken-hearted fools.

*(As **RED** cusses to himself, he makes a line in the dirt with the heal of his boot. He sharpens his bowie knife with slow strokes.)*

KITTY. And no complaints about this cabin, George, where the only way the wind comes through are the *three-inch spaces* in between the boards. Because how should my *husband* know what kind of wood to build with? All those hours in town standing round the whiskey barrel, where I'm sure them men're discussin' which local wood ain't gonna shrink up…

RED. White-livered cowards.

KITTY. Let the Kansas wind blow right into this homestead, I say. Bring with it all the Kansas soil it can carry, I'ma *shovel* that dirt right back outdoors. But, you see, George, it's the *snakes*.

RED. Negro-sympathizin' thieves.

KITTY. Hearing them *slither* underneath my feet just for the joy of it, snaking along the rafters, just waiting to *drop down on me*.

RED. Diggin' them underground railroads.

KITTY. Sleeping with that rifle in between us so I can knock the butt end on the floor before I step out of bed, just to be *ambushed* when I go out back to do my business – their hiss, their rattle – I'm talkin' about –

RED. Those blue-belly, Bible-totin' *Yankees*…

KITTY. The snakes.

RED. Thinkin' they got an abolitionist stake here in Kansas.

KITTY. Because those belly-crawlin' creatures is where I draw the line.

*(**RED** spits across the line in the dirt and walks away. He passes **GEORGE**, who has been standing there listening, even when **KITTY**'s been addressing him, thinking that he's not.)*

GEORGE. I know, Kitty.

*(**GEORGE** is a first-time farmer just finished his morning chores, looking for his coffee.)*

KITTY. Not that Indiana was snake-free land, but these here are –

GEORGE. Kansas snakes.

KITTY. Got one in the coffee pot – all curled up, comfortable-like. Didn't want to disturb 'em.

GEORGE. I'll make the coffee.

KITTY. You make a powerful bad pot of coffee, George.

GEORGE. I know, but this time will be different. This time will be coffee 'n' snake, two different things, mixing and mingling together in that tin pot.

KITTY. George?

GEORGE. Yeah?

KITTY. It's a rattler.

GEORGE. Rattler?

KITTY. Uh-huh.

GEORGE. Well, missus, that's my favorite flavor.

Scene Two: North Meets South

(**HANNAH** *enters, carrying a letter.*)

HANNAH. November 28, 1855. Dear Abigail. We're heeeeere!

*(She dances on **RED**'s line in the dirt, mussing it up, thinking nothing of it.)*

Kansas Territory. Kansas *soil...*

(She reaches down, picks up some of the dirt, puts it in the envelope.)

Enclosed for your perusal or locket, as you see fit. Dear sister, as evidenced by my writing you, we did not get "ambushed by Indians" along the way, although we did get charged double on the riverboat – "Bible surcharge," captain said.

Seems not everyone is as supportive of the New England Immigrant Aid Society as the crowds in Boston at our farewell. I know, little James had the sniffles – again – but you missed a grand leave-taking, Abby – with people holding up dog-eared copies of *Uncle Tom's Cabin* and the look of green envy on Cornelia Ely's face – why, I felt like I was riding off into the sunset on a bronco, instead of getting on a train with a bunch of Christians!

It is true that Papa and Mama, God rest their souls, must have rolled over a few times as their youngest daughter set off to be a schoolteacher on Western frontier. And you did always say: What *good* could come from going to all those Transcendentalist meetings?

But, Abby, it *is* good we're doing here. We're saving this nation from the sin of slavery that's a mark on our souls that no amount of scrubbing can get out. If the Kansas territory is voted into the Union as a slave state, the power split in Washington between North and South will shift – this entire country could be lost.

But, it won't be. We won't let it. First election is tomorrow, to select a territorial delegate – the very first in a long line of ballots leading up to the vote over slavery. And yes, I do know I can't vote myself, and with all the bowie knives around I'm not planning to try. But I can stand here, Abby – my feet planted on this Kansas land – and take up Abolitionist space.

(She seals up the envelope and steps across the patch of dirt where once was **RED***'s line.)*

HANNAH. *(cont.)* Fondly, your sister, Hannah R –

*(***RED*** has appeared, standing just on the other side of the line.)*

RED. Red.

HANNAH. Pardon me.

RED. Introducin' m'self proper. Yer turn. Hannah…

HANNAH. I'm trying to reach –

RED. What?

HANNAH. The *post office*.

RED. Where d'ya think you are?

HANNAH. I need you to move your dirty boots. Sir.

RED. Post office?

HANNAH. You do get *mail* here. I know you do. They said –

RED. No such office.

HANNAH. But this is – town.

RED. Lecompton.

HANNAH. That's right, the second largest –

RED. Mostly saloons – so, I'll jist take that.

HANNAH. No, thank you.

RED. No "sir"?

(He whistles between his teeth.)

My, the manners do go fast in Kansas, don't they girlie…

HANNAH. I'm not a –

RED. That's right, miss, yer an *abolitionist*. Ain't you? Well, I dunno how things go in New England, but down these parts we make proper introductions, Hannah.

HANNAH. You smell like whiskey.

RED. And that's my favorite smell.

HANNAH. And it's still morning.

RED. Don't you know.

(He's got a live one here. **RED** *likes a live one.)*

Edwin. Edwin Redpath.

(He reaches out like to shake her hand, and takes her letter instead.)

But you can call me Red. Hannah...

(She decides she best play along.)

HANNAH. Hannah Rose. Allen.

(He looks at the address on the envelope.)

RED. And I'll jist call you *Boston*, Boston, OK?

HANNAH. OK, I'm just going to post my letter now.

RED. That all yer here for?

HANNAH. Yes. My letter.

RED. Hold up now, Boston, I thought you were here *abolitionizin'*.

*(***HANNAH*** doesn't say anything.)*

I know – that's a biiiig word. Abolitionizin'. Here abolitionizin' this southern territory. Abolitionizin'. Coupla sucks on the whiskey jug, jist rolls off the tongue: abolitionizin'. You're here –

HANNAH. That's *not a word*.

RED. If I say so.

HANNAH. I am an Abolition*ist*. We preach Abolition*ism*. The verb is *preach* and the noun is –

RED. I know what it is, Boston.

HANNAH. I know what you are.

RED. Yer new neighbor.

HANNAH. Border Ruffians they call you.

RED. Half-horse, half-alligator that makes me.

HANNAH. Crossed over the Missouri line.

RED. Whoop louder, jump higher, shoot closer, and git drunker than any man this side o' the Rocky Mountains.

HANNAH. You came here to vote.

RED. And here we go – whoop, whoop – first election's tomorrow.

HANNAH. You don't even *live* here –

RED. Might cast me a dozen ballots 'fore movin' on.

HANNAH. You're – messing with the democratic process!

RED. Jist 'til the whiskey runs dry. Red eye. That's what we call it, Boston. The whiskey.

(He winks as he hands her back her letter. Steps out of her way.)

HANNAH. I – know that.

(And then tells it like it is.)

RED. I know who y'are. You read that Harriet Beecher Stowe one too many times, sittin' blue-bellied with them laced-up boots in front the fire, burnin' wood you never took a hatchet to. And now you think jist because you can tote yer Bible 'cross so many states, you got a right to *mess with* a southern man's liberty. Before *your* whiskey runs out.

You got a whiskey don't ya, Boston? Tell me, what's yer whiskey?

*(**HANNAH** holds her book tight as she moves past him.)*

No *post office*, by the way. Like I said. We ain't that particular, here in the territories. You can leave it there in the store with a man named McGreevy. Tell 'em Red said so, yer letter won't end up rollin' paper fer tobacco. Jist *might* make it back to Boston.

*(**HANNAH** doubles back. Looks him in the eye.)*

HANNAH. Messing with the post is a federal offense, by the way. Even in the territories.

*(She exits with a purpose. **RED** smiles and gives a little whoop as he heads in the other direction.)*

Scene Three: Meet the Neighbors

(Elsewhere that morning, **GEORGE** *and* **JOSIAH**, *the two farmers, stand looking out over the land, tin cups in their hands.)*

GEORGE. Land.

JOSIAH. Good land.

GEORGE. Sure enough.

JOSIAH. Farmin'.

GEORGE. Farmin'.

JOSIAH. Ain't for the faint of heart.

GEORGE. Always said.

JOSIAH. Still. It's there.

GEORGE. The land.

JOSIAH. Might as well farm it.

*(****KITTY*** *appears, holding a coffee pot.)*

KITTY. More coffee, Mr. Nichols?

JOSIAH. Josiah. Only neighbor on the horizon, I best be Josiah.

KITTY. More coffee, Josiah?

JOSIAH. Call me Joe. Never was Josiah in Missouri except to my in-laws.

KITTY. More coffee, Joe?

JOSIAH. Coffee? No, I got to be getting back.

GEORGE. But it's not *on account* of the coffee, that you don't want more coffee?

JOSIAH. On account of the wife of mine. And the winter bein' just 'round the corner.

GEORGE. Because the *coffee* ain't such a bad pot, Joe?

JOSIAH. No, sir, this coffee's right fine.

GEORGE. Got a nice *flavor*. Little something extra…

KITTY. Just *slithers* down your throat.

GEORGE. Kitty, I'll have a touch more.

KITTY. Sure you will.

(She gives him a look as she refills his cup. **GEORGE** *smiles.* **JOSIAH** *puts on his hat.)*

JOSIAH. Well, I best be going.

KITTY. Your wife is well, Joe?

JOSIAH. Louisa. She is.

KITTY. Tell me, does she mind the dirt?

JOSIAH. She's always minding the dirt. Minding the children. Minding the cooking and the washing – keeps the place right clean.

KITTY. But this Kansas dirt.

JOSIAH. Oh, we had dirt back in Missouri.

KITTY. But blowing inside, through the spaces in between the boards?

JOSIAH. We don't have much in the way of spaces. Built with pine.

KITTY. Did ya. With pine.

JOSIAH. Sealed up the few spaces, here 'n' there.

KITTY. Hear that, George?

GEORGE. I'm standing right here, Kitty.

KITTY. Drinkin' yer coffee.

JOSIAH. Show you anytime, George, just come 'round the farm.

GEORGE. I'd appreciate that. And – many thanks, Joe. For bringing by those fence posts.

JOSIAH. Got to fence off your claim, now. Use as many as you like, I finished mine up last week.

GEORGE. Did ya.

KITTY. He did.

JOSIAH. Well, I best be going. Louisa.

KITTY. Sounds like Louisa's – quite the homesteader, minding all that she does.

JOSIAH. Oh, she is. Canning this time of year, too. Drying the herbs she planted out back.

KITTY. Any tobacco? That's my favorite herb.

JOSIAH. No, the – uh, kitchen herbs. Dill and what not.
KITTY. Kitchen herbs.
JOSIAH. Oh, and she's got another one on the way, now.
KITTY. And how many does that make?
JOSIAH. Three girls and a boy. Baby makes five.
KITTY. All them alive now, too?
GEORGE. *Kitty...*
KITTY. Well, you best be getting back then.
JOSIAH. Many thanks for the coffee, Mrs. Clarke.

(**JOSIAH** *hands* **KITTY** *his cup.*)

George.
GEORGE. Joe.
KITTY. It's Kittson.
JOSIAH. Many thanks, Kittson.
KITTY. Kitty. Like the feline. Only neighbor on the horizon, you best call me Kitty, Joe.

(**JOSIAH** *nods and exits.*)

Hear that, George.
GEORGE. I'm standing right here.

(*He drinks his coffee.*)

KITTY. Seems children are being born. Right here in Kansas.
GEORGE. Seems that way.
KITTY. Seems some farmers got their fences up. Houses sealed –
GEORGE. You heard it. Right from the farmer's mouth.
KITTY. They got kitchen herbs.
GEORGE. And what use have *we* got for kitchen herbs?
KITTY. I'm just saying, George. And I'm just wondering what're you doing just standing there?
GEORGE. Right now? I'm finishing my morning coffee. And I'm looking out over the land, which is *our land*. And I'm thinking on the moon.
KITTY. Of course you are. On the moon.

GEORGE. The Kansas moon, Kittson. Did you not see it last night?

KITTY. No, George, I did not see *the moon.*

GEORGE. Because I thought you did. When I looked over at you, thought I saw your eyes out the window. And if you were looking anywhere *near* that window, you could see nothing but the moon.

KITTY. I was listening for rattles. As in rattlers. As in – *the snakes.*

GEORGE. They say the Kansas moon's so beautiful, it's like the moon over Venice, Italy.

KITTY. As if any of these Missourians have ever set foot in –

GEORGE. Don't have to. Just look out the window. Like you were doing last night.

KITTY. I was someplace else.

GEORGE. Looking at the moon…

KITTY. Yes, *the moon* – it fills up the whole darned window, how could I not see –

GEORGE. That moon that could inspire poetry and Italian love songs –

KITTY. But *my mind* was someplace else. Someplace in between Kansas and Indiana, in a field, where the ground is going to be getting cold. Where that mound of dirt has long dried from the tears we watered it with, because what can you do but water for an hour or two, and then get back into your wagon and move on.

(From the pocket of her apron, **KITTY** *takes out a wooden horse, a child's toy.)*

GEORGE. Wasn't nothing more we could do.

KITTY. I know that.

GEORGE. This is a *good* place here, Kitty.

KITTY. I know, George.

GEORGE. The opportunities. We went west, just like your parents and mine. And today, west means Kansas. What was there for us in Indiana?

KITTY. Nothing. And you know I'd follow you to the dead end of the earth, George Clarke. But sometimes I wish you wouldn't just lie there, looking over my shoulder like you could make out what *might be* reflected in my eyes.

GEORGE. Your back's beautiful in the moonlight.

KITTY. I expect that's true. But my front terrain's got a little more to offer. If you remember.

(She stands with her back to him. There is some distance between them.)

KITTY. George, I love you. I do. Like a –

GEORGE. Wild cat.

KITTY. But I lack the *confidence* in you when it comes to the farming. You put the two of us together, George – between us both we don't know three beans about turning this land into farm.

GEORGE. We got the belief.

KITTY. In *what*?

GEORGE. Kansas.

KITTY. Kansas.

GEORGE. We can do this, Kitty. Together, we'll do it. And it will be *good* here. I know it will. This is good land. Just give it a little time.

KITTY. And how much is a little time? Because we only got *a little time* before winter –

GEORGE. Time enough for me to get up that fence. Time enough for you to be makin' friends with the snakes, or at least showin' 'em that we're here to stay. That they can slither around all they want, we ain't gonna pay them no mind, because we're busy here drinking our coffee, looking at the moon, planting our feet in this soil – making this land here our own.

KITTY. Kansas.

GEORGE. Kansas.

KITTY. Wild cat, huh?

GEORGE. Always said.

KITTY. Uh-huh.

GEORGE. Kitty, you and me – the two of us together – we got all the time in the world.

KITTY. As long as we got the time for sealing up the spaces in the walls of this cabin.

GEORGE. Tomorrow.

KITTY. Tomorrow *morning*.

GEORGE. First thing – I'll stop in at Joe's on my way into town.

KITTY. *Town* – ?

GEORGE. Lecompton.

KITTY. And George Clarke, what business have you got going to *town* tomorrow?

GEORGE. Got the business of voting.

KITTY. And what do you care to vote?

GEORGE. I care because this land is going to be our state.

KITTY. You don't give a boot about politics!

GEORGE. It ain't politics, it's my right.

KITTY. That's right – yer God-given right to stand in front of McGreevy's store –

GEORGE. *Kansas* is home now.

KITTY. Shooting the moon, shooting the red eye with those *men*…

GEORGE. And I won't have any of 'em telling us how things are gonna be here.

(He hands her his empty coffee cup, going to get at those fence posts. She calls after him.)

KITTY. Uh-huh. And when's it gonna occur to you, George, to bring a jug of that whiskey home?

Scene Four: Any Three Men

(Nighttime. We hear the sound of crickets, and of horses riding on a dirt road. The horses stop. **TWO MEN** *enter from one direction – a third is heading the opposite way. We almost can't see them in the shadows, but their voices carry through the night.)*

RED. Where're you going?

MAN FROM LAWRENCE. *(played by* **JOSIAH***)* I'm going home.

MAN FROM LECOMPTON. *(played by* **GEORGE***)* Where're you coming from?

MAN FROM LAWRENCE. From town.

MAN FROM LECOMPTON. What's going on in town?

MAN FROM LAWRENCE. Nothing in particular.

MAN FROM LECOMPTON. Nothing in particular, hey?

MAN FROM LAWRENCE. That's right.

RED. Not what we heard.

MAN FROM LECOMPTON. Lawrence.

MAN FROM LAWRENCE. That's right. Lawrence.

MAN FROM LECOMPTON. Where all them abolitionists're at.

MAN FROM LAWRENCE. I'm no abolitionist.

RED. You ain't proslavery either, if you been in Lawrence.

MAN FROM LAWRENCE. I'm going home, to chop winter wood for my family. What's it to you?

MAN FROM LECOMPTON. We're from Lecompton.

MAN FROM LAWRENCE. What's going on in Lecompton?

MAN FROM LECOMPTON. That would be celebratin' our victry over the vote.

MAN FROM LAWRENCE. Still?

RED. Still.

MAN FROM LECOMPTON. Better git used to it. Since we'll be takin' all them elections, no matter the numbers.

RED. We got our own particular way of countin', don't you know.

MAN FROM LECOMPTON. And us Ruffians like wipin' clean a bloody knife jist as much as much as we like votin'.

(They breathe. The night is heavy.)

RED. My, that's a nice holster ya got there, hey? Shiny and new.

MAN FROM LAWRENCE. I got to be getting home to my family. Gentlemen.

MAN FROM LECOMPTON. Ain't nothin' *gentle* 'bout us men in Lecompton.

RED. Ain't but 12 miles from our town to yours, Lawrence.

Scene Five: The Women

(**HANNAH** *knocks on the door. She is freezing. She knocks again.* **KITTY**, *with an Indian blanket around herself, answers. Two different kinds of women, standing eye to eye.*)

KITTY. Who're you? Three parts cold, one part stupid...

(**KITTY** *grabs shivering* **HANNAH** *and pulls her inside, wraps the blanket around her.*)

Plannin' to freeze outside our door, so we got to *step over* your body all winter, get rid of it come spring. If spring ever comes. Forget it – it ain't coming. So, what've we got here?

(**KITTY** *goes through* **HANNAH**'s *sack while* **HANNAH** *epistles.*)

HANNAH. Dear Abigail. I am sending you this letter so you won't be alarmed when you hear the Coltons have return to Boston. And the Rotters. And the Mannings, who envisioned me as the first schoolteacher in Kansas, but who packed it up after the lesson they learned from the first election:

Over 5,000 votes for the pro-slavery representative – but Abby, there're less than 3,000 registered voters in the entire territory! And something about those Southern *gentlemen* with their bowie knives, checking every vote *before* it was cast, that tended to scare off the abolitionist male.

Not me. I'm not scared, Abby. I – miss you. But I'm not leaving until the final election to decide the question of slavery, no matter how many Kansas winters I have to endure. And though I can't vote, I will write letters to every abolitionist newspaper this side of –

(**KITTY** *has unpacked the entire contents of* **HANNAH**'s *sack. Only books. Checks again.*)

KITTY. Where's the rest of it?
HANNAH. That's what I got. My books.

(**HANNAH** *stands by her books.* **KITTY** *seems confused.*)

KITTY. But – what *for*?

HANNAH. To read.

KITTY. In Kansas?

HANNAH. Re-read, actually – been through them all.

KITTY. Here I was thinking portable firewood. Re-*read*.

HANNAH. Read them *over* –

KITTY. I know what it *means*, doll, I just – don't understand. That's all you got with you?

HANNAH. That's all I could carry.

KITTY. Where're your people?

HANNAH. They – had to go. Back to Boston.

KITTY. Boston. So you're one of those.

HANNAH. And they weren't *my people*. I was only living under their roof and caring for their young ones until the schoolhouse –

KITTY. Where's your man?

HANNAH. I haven't got one.

KITTY. Then whose bright idea was it to come to Kansas?

HANNAH. I'm here to –

KITTY. I know, I know – I've heard what *you people* are here for. Causing trouble.

HANNAH. Where's your man?

KITTY. My old man's chopping wood. He'll be back. Unless he's froze. He's probably froze.

HANNAH. And you've got – no children?

KITTY. What's it to you?

HANNAH. I just meant – it's only the *two* of you – here in this whole cabin?

KITTY. Just us two.

HANNAH. It's a nice cabin –

KITTY. We had a little girl. Flora. She died, on the road to Kansas.

HANNAH. Oh. I. I'm –

KITTY. And this cabin ain't what I expect you'd call *nice*.

HANNAH. No, it is, really, it's –

KITTY. Warm enough. Just barely. If you don't open the door. In fact, I think you knocked on the wrong door. We ain't yer kind, miss. And don't think we haven't noticed how you all look down your noses at our rough manners. We got no interest in Bibles here –

HANNAH. Please.

KITTY. Just trying to keep our feet from freezing.

HANNAH. I'm just – cold. I've got no place else I can go. Not until the spring melts the road from here to Lawrence. And I am *cold*.

(They look one another in the eye.)

KITTY. Next farm over's Josiah Nichols' place. Sure you'd be much more comfortable waiting out the winter there. I'm sure they got – jars and jars of preserves. You must have seen their cabin from the road, all that smoke out their functioning chimney – don't see why you can't knock there.

HANNAH. Because they're proslavery.

KITTY. We're no abolitionists.

HANNAH. I know. But you don't want slavery in this state either. You folks are Free Soil.

KITTY. What's it to you?

HANNAH. Everything.

(A knock at the door. The women look at each other. Insistent knocking. KITTY answers. RED is standing there. Freezing, but not showing it.)

KITTY. Thought you said you haven't got a man –

HANNAH. Stop following me!

RED. Jist makin' sure ya didn't freeze, Boston.

HANNAH. As evidenced by my standing here, I *didn't*.

KITTY. What've we got here?

HANNAH. Border Ruffian. The kind you secure your doors against. Three parts danger, one part –

RED. Whiskey.

HANNAH. What are you still doing in Kansas? I imagine you cast yourself enough votes in the last election –

RED. To last me through the winter – that's right, we took that vote like a two-dollar whore, and now I'm lookin' forward to the next one –

KITTY. *Whiskey*, you said?

> *(***RED** *slowly raises the jug he's carrying.* **KITTY** *eyes that jug of whiskey.)*

In that case – not that either of you're stayin' long enough to wipe yer boots – we might as well finish this in front the fire.

Scene Six: One Jug of Whiskey, One Greasy Pack of Cards

(Later that night, **HANNAH**, **KITTY**, **RED**, **GEORGE**, *and* **JOE** *play poker and drink whiskey. They've been at it for a while.* **KITTY** *gives a whoop-whoop and does a dance over her winning hand.* **GEORGE** *and* **RED** *sit across from one another, doing shots.* **JOE** *pours into one set of cups, and then the next, while they struggle to keep up.* **HANNAH** *counts off the shots.)*

HANNAH. One!

(Shoot.)

Two!

(Shoot.)

Three!

*(***KITTY*** grabs the jug from ***JOE*** and takes a swig.)*

KITTY. Deal 'em up, Red! This Kitty wants to win again…
GEORGE. Oh, you do, do you?
KITTY. I ain't lying. Not yet anyway.

*(***KITTY*** sits on ***GEORGE***'s lap.)*

GEORGE. And what're you planning on winning?
KITTY. The moon.
GEORGE. Well, you're sitting in my territory now, no telling what'll happen.

*(***GEORGE*** plants a kiss on her. Like it would melt all the snow in Kansas.)*

JOE. Shuffle, Mr. Red.
RED. Need another shot to shuffle.
JOE. I'll just – take that.

*(***JOE*** takes the jug from ***KITTY*** who is occupied with other matters. Pours ***RED*** another.)*

HANNAH. One shot for the shuffler!
GEORGE. Go on, Joe, have another yourself.

JOE. Oh, I best be going.

KITTY. But it's medicine, Joe.

JOE. I don't know…

HANNAH. The word's *medicinal*, although –

KITTY. Whatever she said.

JOE. Louisa, *she* said –

GEORGE. She'd want you take your medicine –

KITTY. Like a good farmer.

(**JOE** *takes his medicine.*)

JOE. She said, just bring 'em what I canned, so they don't *starve* before they *freeze*.

KITTY. Well, ain't she neighborly.

(**KITTY** *does a shot.* **GEORGE** *pushes a cup towards* **HANNAH**.)

GEORGE. Go on, miss, your turn.

KITTY. Doll-face don't touch the stuff.

HANNAH. I never said –

GEORGE. Maybe she's just pacing herself. So she don't fall over. Which I seen happen.

(**GEORGE** *winks.*)

KITTY. Don't you know these abolitionists preach the temperance?

HANNAH. I just – don't think it's actually *medicinal*.

JOE. No need to explain, miss.

KITTY. And here she is with us drinkin', gamblin' heathens.

JOE. You *should* be scared of the red eye.

HANNAH. I'm not scared of a drink.

KITTY. Put hair on your chest. You wanna see my hairy…

(**KITTY** *starts to unbutton.*)

GEORGE. *Kitty…*

HANNAH. As evidenced by my being in Kansas, I am not *afraid* of…

(HANNAH *meets eyes with* RED, *who looks up from his shuffling.*)

RED. Go on, Boston.

HANNAH. What I mean is: I ain't afraid of no whiskey. Jist have yer ol' man filler up, missus, I reckon I'll shoot this here red eye down.

(GEORGE *pours it.* HANNAH *does her first shot. Coughs. The stuff is truly awful.* GEORGE *and* JOE *whoop.*)

GEORGE. That's a little miss.

JOE. Liquid danger.

(HANNAH *holds out her glass.* GEORGE *refills it. She raises her glass.*)

HANNAH. Dear Abigail. We got this thing here in Kansas called the *red eye*. Quite different than that *pink eye* your little James had.

(HANNAH *downs shot number two.*)

KITTY. Something to write home about, ain't it? A little taste of the frontier, before you git on back home to Boston.

(As KITTY *throws back another...*)

HANNAH. Who said I'm going back?

(KITTY *turns to* RED, *who continues his well-oiled shuffle.*)

KITTY. And *you* – you got the fingers for the cards, don't you?

GEORGE. Red, they call you.

RED. That's right.

GEORGE. Where'd you come from?

RED. From town.

GEORGE. What's going on in town?

RED. Nothing in particular.

GEORGE. Nothing in particular, hey?

KITTY. He's from Missouri, Georgie, don't you know. Just like our neighbor Joe here, except he hasn't been bridled by Louisa. He's one of those –

HANNAH. Border Ruffians, causing trouble in Lecompton.

JOE. My Lou-Lou could tell what county in Missouri, just by the way you say *cow*.

RED. I bin 'round.

HANNAH. Around the *whiskey barrel*, you mean –

RED. I mean *Texas*. Fightin'.

GEORGE. What for?

RED. To fight. To have somethin' to cuss about when we're throwin' cards in the saloon, pissin' round the campfire. Road on down to Mexico – goin' days through that desert, not knowin' where my next drop was comin' from, never sure if that last one *was* my last. Land like you never seen.

Not like Missouri or Kansas, where it spreads out before you like a loose woman, but land with sharp red edges and plants that bite you back. Where that scorpion in yer boots come morning and that buzzard's been circlin' you all day are yer only God-given companions.

And the Rio Grande runs East-West, jist like our Missouri – but it runs thicker. And when some man calls you Eddie, shortenin' yer Edwin Redpath, it won't be out his mouth twice before he hits the ground. So, that's right. They call me *Red* now. Jist like that land. Like my hands after a good fight, before I wipe them clean and pick up the cards.

KITTY. And what do you do now, Red?

RED. I deal.

*(**RED** deals the cards.)*

GEORGE. Now he does whatever David Atchison says.

JOE. Our good senator from Missouri.

GEORGE. Who should *stay* in Missouri, mind his own state.

HANNAH. Old Bourbon they call him, Atchison –

GEORGE. Says he'd rather see Kansas sunk to the bottom of Hell than become a free state.

HANNAH. Because he *drinks* so much.

RED. That sounds like our man Atchison.

GEORGE. Sounds to me like a problem.

KITTY. Well, then.

GEORGE. Especially when I ain't allowed to vote otherwise.

KITTY. Looks here like we all got our cards spread out before us.

JOE. Clean shuffle.

(They each pick up their cards. **HANNAH***'s emboldened by the drink.)*

RED. God knows what each of us've been dealt.

HANNAH. Can we please leave *God* out of the card playing?

KITTY. You're the one who brought 'em along, all them Bibles –

HANNAH. *One* Bible –

RED. Sounds like your hand needs a prayer.

HANNAH. Well, then. Maybe you read me wrong.

KITTY. Are we wagering?

GEORGE. Haven't got a thing.

*(***GEORGE*** throws down his cards.)*

RED. None of us got a thing to wager.

KITTY. The women, loose or otherwise, *always* got something.

HANNAH. The hair on our chest.

JOE. Well, I haven't even got that.

*(***JOE*** throws down his hand.* **GEORGE** *pours* **JOE** *a shot.)*

I best be…

GEORGE. For the road, Joe.

JOE. Oh, almost forgot. Mrs. Clarke –

KITTY. *Kitty*, Joe…

KITTY & JOE. Like the feline.

(**JOE** *takes out a small packet tucked inside his shirt.*)

JOE. This here's from my Louisa.
GEORGE. Tobacco.
KITTY. For me?
JOE. Had a bit tucked away. Didn't even think Louisa knew about it, but she did, and she's making me share. Says it's the only way we're all gonna make it here in Kansas.
KITTY. That's right neighborly of her, Josiah. That it is.
GEORGE. To Lou-Lou!

(**KITTY** *kisses* **JOSIAH** *on the cheek.* **GEORGE** *pours them all shots, as they see* **JOE** *off.*)

(**HANNAH** *and* **RED** *are still in the game.*)

HANNAH. They're drinking all your whiskey.
RED. You drank some yerself.
HANNAH. Is that what you want, get them drunk, so you can make off with the stove?
RED. That what yer bettin' on?

(*She giggles. She's drunk.*)

HANNAH. *You* – holding the *stove* trying not to burn your *hands* – couple of *logs* in your *boots*.
RED. You still don't know why I came here, do you?
HANNAH. I think you're sweet on me.
RED. And what do *you* know from sweet?
HANNAH. Rock candy. In a paper bag.
RED. Yer bluffin'.
HANNAH. Am I?
RED. Boston, I been to Mexico and back. That jug of red eye? Jist bought yer winter quarters.
HANNAH. I don't need you looking after me, you know. I came a long way – *on my own* – and I'm not stopping now.
RED. How far will you go?
HANNAH. I don't know. Try me.

(They eye one another over the cards.)

RED. I saw them leave you off. Loaded-up wagon, youngins screaming in back. Dropping you there in the middle of town. At least they had the sense not to leave you in whatever poor excuse for a cabin they were vacating. But the whole operation didn't strike me as particularly *Christian*, those abolitionists, leaving you alone here in Kansas.

HANNAH. I wanted to stay.

RED. And don't think I don't know, Boston, why you couldn't stay on in town. Workin' for McCreevy for your room and board, when that man's got three sets of hands, one for each of 'em pretty girls he's got workin' behind the counter of that store. I know why you set off on that road, middle of winter, nothin' but a sack of *books*.

HANNAH. That's my whiskey. My Shakespeare, Thoreau, *Uncle Tom's* – that's keeping me going.

RED. Well, my whiskey's *whiskey*. And that's keeping you alive.

HANNAH. Why are you doing this?

RED. Thought I was sweet on you.

HANNAH. Go back to Missouri, Red.

RED. I can't go back. Got nothin' in Missouri but trouble.

HANNAH. I got nothin' in Boston either.

RED. Yer kinda nothin' writes you boring letters. My kind of nothin' gets me killed. So I thought I'd stick 'round Kansas. For the fight. Because we *are* going to fight, Boston. Soon as the snow melts. You standin' on your side. Me standin' right here. All this sweet land in between us, ready to bleed.

HANNAH. You think you know who I am. You think you can watch me and follow me, and that you *know* me, but you don't.

(She lays down her hand. Can't help but smile at it.)

See? You don't know what I've got, mister. I tasted blood before. My finger's been pricked. And I ain't scared of a little red.

Scene Seven: Kansas-Style Lovin'

(**KITTY** *enters a dark room, carrying a rifle. She knocks the butt of the rifle on the ground. Takes a few cautious steps. Knocks it again.*)

KITTY. Shoo! Just – shoo! All of you, leave us alone tonight, you got that? No rattles at all, nothing moving but what's in this sweet bed. Because he's mine tonight and I'm his, and you got no business slithering about, distracting a woman from the *honey* at hand – and I'm talkin' the whole sweet pot. So much honey, we could spread it over us and still have some leftover for a late spring. See, this here's *my* territory, you rattle-asses, and tonight there is nothing outside this room, these loving arms, and that moon.

(**KITTY** *stands at the window, bathing in the moon. She lifts the rifle and aims at it.* **GEORGE** *enters and watches her.*)

No, not even you.

(**KITTY** *mimes shooting the moon.* **GEORGE** *plays the now-empty whiskey jug. As he plays, he comes up behind* **KITTY**. *He sings to the tune of "Campton Racetrack"*)

GEORGE.
FARMER GEORGE HAS A WIFE KIT-TY,
OH YEAH, OH YEAH
WOULD LIKE TO HAVE HER ON MY KNEE,
OH YEAH DO ONE DAY
OH, WOULD YOU SEE HER BACK!
WHICH I'D LIKE TO HAVE…

(**GEORGE** *takes hold of* **KITTY**'s *ass.*)

BUT TURN HER AROUND AND YOU WILL SEE
LOOK, THERE'S A PUSSY…CAT.

KITTY. It's like I'm some princess of Venice, and you're wooing me under the Italian moon.

GEORGE. What moon?

KITTY. Oh, Georgie, I like you playing on that jug.

(**GEORGE** *drops the jug. He puts his hands on her.*)

GEORGE. I like your land.

KITTY. I like your hands playing on my lands.

GEORGE. You're no Italian princess.

(**KITTY** *purrs.*)

Wouldn't have you any other way.

KITTY. Thought you'd be having me every which way.

GEORGE. That what you thought?

KITTY. Uh-huh. Farmer George.

GEORGE. Yeah?

KITTY. Let's have another one.

GEORGE. Another –

KITTY. Yeah.

GEORGE. Oh, Kitty, we said –

KITTY. We can't wait until we got a functioning farm, because –

GEORGE. At least until we know it's safe here.

KITTY. It'll never be safe.

GEORGE. But for a *child*, Kitty, we –

KITTY. I think we got everything we need…

(*With a smile, she feels to make sure. He moves away from her.*)

GEORGE. We – no – I can't – do it. Kitty, you know I don't know what I'm doing here. Yes, I'm a believer in the land, but I don't know three beans about farming it, and until I learn – I can't love another one, just to have that little one taken away.

I think on her, too. Not when I look at the moon, but

the sun – setting over the land. Think of our Flora lying in that lone field halfway between Indiana and Kansas. And I can't feel like it's my fault all over again.

KITTY. What about me?

GEORGE. You're the strong one.

KITTY. But this is what you *do*. Try again. Make a new start. Isn't that what we're doing here? Hey.

(She brings him back.)

That's why we're here. Come on, George. Look at me. It's just me. We can do this. Together. See? All you got to do is love me. Leave *Kansas* out of it. Leave it all alone. Just – love me.

(He looks at her. Picks her up. This is a new beginning.)

Scene Eight: The Morning After & the Morning Before

(**HANNAH** *stands in the cabin, the Indian blanket wrapped around her, reading from a copy of* Uncle Tom's Cabin. **KITTY** *enters.*)

KITTY. Still here.

HANNAH. I got some water.

(**KITTY** *goes to pour herself some.*)

It froze.

(**KITTY** *puts down the kettle and sits, as* **HANNAH** *puts the blanket around* **KITTY**.)

Your man's out welcoming the morning, that's what he said...

(**KITTY** *smiles to herself. She fills her pipe with her new tobacco.*)

But I hear chopping. I think that's what he meant. Chopping wood – I could be gone before he gets back.

KITTY. That wouldn't be very Christian of us, now would it? Not very neighborly either, not that I'm aiming at either one, just trying to keep my George happy, because he makes me very happy, and George says you can stay.

Can't say you take up much space. Seems you can fetch water. Just see you don't hog the liquor – don't even dream of touching my tobacco. Keep those books of yours stacked in the corner, keep that Ruffian with the greasy cards – who I don't know *how* you got mixed up with – outside shooting range. Unless he's got a fresh jug.

And most of all, keep them abolitionist ideas and strange Boston habits to yerself. Don't stand so straight and tall. Sit with your legs planted firmly to the earth. And earn your keep by killing at least three snakes a week. So. What're we gonna call you?

HANNAH. My sister calls me Hannah Rose.

(**KITTY** *lights her pipe, puffs on it.*)

Last night I dreamt I was crossing the Missouri River. Jumping from ice floe to ice floe, and it was so dark I couldn't see the other side. So I just kept jumping.

But then the sun rose – a powerful sun, reflecting off of the surface of the ice – and it warmed my back, and the river flowed faster and faster, and soon I was riding that Missouri like a prophet – my arms raised, my voice squealing in my ears.

KITTY. That'd be the red eye.

HANNAH. Then the ice below my feet started to melt. Disappearing at a startling rate, and I knew that it would soon be gone, but my heart kept on beating steady, slowed even – I raised my skirts to my knees and fixed my eyes on the horizon. And when I awoke, I was here.

KITTY. Kansas.

HANNAH. What does it mean, Kitty – my dream?

KITTY. I know the answer ain't in here.

(**KITTY** *takes the copy of* Uncle Tom's Cabin *that* **HANNAH** *has been re-reading.*)

HANNAH. But that's –

KITTY. The word of God?

HANNAH. Harriet Beecher Stowe.

KITTY. A woman. Even still.

(**KITTY** *stacks the book with the others in the corner.*)

HANNAH. But my dream –

KITTY. It means – Hannah Rose – that *springtime* will come.

(*And it does.* **KITTY** *removes the blanket from her shoulders.* **HANNAH** *opens a window.* **GEORGE** *enters and pours coffee from the pot that was previously frozen.*)

GEORGE. Popular sovereignty. That means *we* the people of Kansas are to decide if this here be a slave state or a free state.

HANNAH. That's what the Kansas-Nebraska Act says.

GEORGE. A question of the vote, which is a question of *rights*, the way I see it.

KITTY. Well, it ain't a question of the *slaves*, because I never seen a-one in Kansas.

HANNAH. But it's all about the slaves!

KITTY. Then explain to me why Josiah's pro-slavery when he hasn't got any slaves, never will, unless you count *him* indentured to Louisa.

GEORGE. It's the peculiar Southern *institution* of slavery –

HANNAH. Which is a scourge on the soul of our entire nation!

KITTY. Our nation's soul? What Christians do you think you're preaching to in this house?

(**KITTY** *folds up the winter blanket.* **GEORGE** *and* **HANNAH** *sit at the table.*)

GEORGE. Look, Joe's from Missiouri, and the Missiourians are pro-slavery, because that's what they got in Missouri – slaves – and they want to keep it that way, and frankly that's fine by me –

HANNAH. Not by me.

KITTY. Heard ya the first time, doll.

GEORGE. But these Southerners are trying to *spread* slavery – thinking they can just come here to Kansas and *take away* the political liberties of me and everyone else, when the majority of us settlers are Free Soilers.

HANNAH. They're messing with the democratic process.

GEORGE. Don't you know it, miss – and that's against the Constitution, against the War for Independence and the spirit of our forefathers – downright un-American, messin' with the popular sovereignty.

HANNAH. After we moved here to *vote* Kansas in as a free state.

(**KITTY** *takes the toy horse out of her pocket.*)

KITTY. No, *we* didn't. We moved here for a better life for our children, if you remember.

(**KITTY** *hands* **GEORGE** *the horse. He remembers carving it. Gifting it. He holds it.*)

HANNAH. And I moved here to make Kansas a free state. I'm not forgetting –

KITTY. Uh-huh, how you abolitionists are here turning up trouble. And don't think I don't know, Hannah Rose, how you been burnin' down our candles writing letters to your sympathizin' newspapers –

HANNAH. Our letters are winning supporters back East –

KITTY. And, George, you might recall that "meddlesome Yankees" was a phrase you yourself used more than once –

GEORGE. I know – and you'll have to excuse that, Hannah – but we're fighting on the same side now, Kitty. The abolitionists got their reasons, and us Free Soilers got ours. Those slave plantations take over the land and prevent working people like us from having our own homestead. And with slavery comes the Negroes, and I don't want them black people here populating my state.

HANNAH. I'm sorry but can't excuse that.

KITTY. And last I checked, women *can't* vote – and men sure can *talk*, can't they?

GEORGE. This ain't just talk, Kitty.

KITTY. And George I don't know what you've got to talk *about* considering you know less about politics than you do about farming.

GEORGE. I know I got rights, Kitty. That's my belief, and I know it in my heart. And I know it ain't right, what they're trying to do here in Kansas. Because I'm here working this land, and that gives me certain rights to decide the fate of this here land. This is our America, and we got a right to it. It's only *right*. That's why I'm standing up.

KITTY. Because they didn't count your vote, that's what this is all about.

GEORGE. Because when they opened up my ballot before it ever reached that box, and fixed it to the wall with a bloody knife, there wasn't a thing I could do but stand there.

HANNAH. It shouldn't even be a vote.

KITTY. So, you want it to be – *a fight?*

HANNAH. It's above a vote. This is *slavery* – a question of moral principle – it's a question of –

KITTY. Don't even say –

HANNAH. God.

KITTY. Because I don't believe it, doll, even if it is Sunday.

GEORGE. It's a question of men.

KITTY. The *men* – I believe that, because it's always the men.

GEORGE. A man's liberty –

HANNAH. The *black* man's –

GEORGE. *My* liberty.

KITTY. Spoken like a man.

GEORGE. A man making this a free territory for free white people. Spoken like *your* old man, Kitty. Thinking about you, like I always am because you know I can't help myself…

KITTY. Georgie –

GEORGE. Thinking about the future of this country for *our* children – that's why this fight matters.

(**GEORGE** *hands the toy horse back to* **KITTY**.)

KITTY. This *farm* is what matters. So why don't you all farm the farms, and not worry about who's preaching what about slavery or drinkin' in the name of Southern pride –

GEORGE. If Atchison has his way, and turns this Kansas into another Missouri –

KITTY. Then our children will grow up with a funny way of saying "cow."

HANNAH. It would mean they won. That slavery would move into the North. That the pro-slavery forces in Washington would have the upper hand – that this country would be lost.

GEORGE. And we're not supposed to say a damned thing about it. That *unlawfully* elected proslavery legislature's moved right here to Lecompton. They passed some new Bogus Laws – a free man in Kansas now can't even write or speak against slaveholding.

KITTY. Amen to that.

GEORGE. No man is gonna tell me I can't speak my mind, Kittson.

KITTY. That's right, a *woman* is, telling you to just keep your mind to yourself, George Clarke, or at least steer clear of Lecompton – because you know there's plenty of men in that town just itchin' to enforce them new laws, bogus or otherwise.

Scene Nine: Two Sides

(HANNAH bathes in a last moment of sunshine.)

HANNAH. May 21, 1856. Dear Abigail. Yesterday, Kansas was – perfect. For one moment the winds and the sun conspired to give us the most beautiful weather in the world. And the earth sent up the wildflowers, and the snakes all decided to head for the prairie, and the Clarkes opened up their cabin and we scrubbed out every last mark of dirt. It wasn't clean like Boston-clean, with its feather-dusted porcelain, but we *owned* it. And somehow that made it taste sweeter.

(And then RED enters. He plays not himself, but proslavery leader DAVID ATCHISON, delivering a speech to a crowd of Ruffians.)

ATCHISON. *(played by RED)* Boys, this day I am a Kickapoo Ranger, by God, if my name isn't David Atchison, more affectionately known to you as Old Bourbon. And today is the happiest day of my life.

HANNAH. But today, Kansas is – hot. Heat of summer, already in the month of May – that drop there on the page is my sweat. For days it's been nearing a boil in the free-state town of Lawrence. Hundreds of Border Ruffians have been seen silhouetted on the crest of the hill, just outside town. Gathering there. Today they rode in.

ATCHISON. This day we have entered Lawrence with Southern Rights inscribed on our banner, and not one damned abolitionist dared to fire a gun. We have taught the damned abolitionists a Southern lesson that they will remember until the day they die.

HANNAH. When we heard news of smoke rising out of Lawrence, George Clarke got his horse and headed straight for Lecompton. Said he had to find out what was happening.

Abigail, I don't know what's to happen here in –

ATCHISON. Now, boys, we will go in again.

HANNAH. No, I'd be lying if I wrote that.

ATCHISON. And, boys, *ladies* should – and I hope will be – respected by every gentleman…

HANNAH. As evidenced by my shaking hand, I do know what's going to happen here in Kansas.

ATCHISON. But when a woman takes upon herself the garb of a soldier by carrying a Sharpe's rifle? Trample her under your feet as you would a snake. If one man or woman dare stand before you, blow them to hell with a chunk of cold lead.

HANNAH. And I say, let it happen.

*(**ATCHISON** removes his hat and coat, and is transformed to **RED**. He looks directly at **HANNAH**. They stand with distance in between them.)*

RED. Dear Boston. I'd be lyin' if I said you weren't *on my mind*. As we entered Lawrence. Rode right up to the office of the *Kansas Free State*. That's a newspaper office, don't you know, right here in Kansas territory.

*(**RED** laughs. **HANNAH** stands, poker-faced, meeting his gaze.)*

Not anymore. Took an axe to that printing press – that *abolitionizin'* press. Tossed the half-printed late edition out the window, papers scattered about the prairie for a mile 'round.

And then we got back on our horses and road to the office of the *Herald of Freedom*. Where we found boxes and boxes of – see, Boston, this is where I think on you – some 300 books. Jist arrived. Thick covers. Pretty typeset pages, only one in every half-dozen were Bibles. We took them all, *hacked* them with our *sabers*.

*(**HANNAH** walks right up to **RED**. She spits on the ground in next to him. With her boot, she mixes the dirt with her spit.)*

And then we marched out of there, each one of us carrying a stabbed-through book at the end of his blade. Why? Because that's what us Ruffians do.

(HANNAH *spreads the mud on her cheeks in stripes like war paint.*)

RED. *(cont.)* Jist like you abolitionists write *nice* letters, don't I know. Now that I *know* yer hand. Got it right here in my pocket.

(RED *takes a letter out from* HANNAH *out of his pocket. He stands close enough for her to smell the whiskey on his breath.*)

And yer welcome for that whiskey if what you were aimin' to say was thanks.

Don't say I never wrote back, Boston. Don't think I weren't thinking on you too.

Signed: Edwin Redpath. More affectionately known to you as: Red.

(RED *exits, leaving* HANNAH *there, as* KITTY *and* JOSIAH *enter.* JOSIAH *carries nearly unconscious* GEORGE, *who bleeds from a deep gash on the side of his head.*)

KITTY. George, oh God, George…

JOSIAH. I couldn't leave him there.

KITTY. Where – where did –

JOSIAH. In town.

KITTY. Hannah, get water!

JOSIAH. We were in Lecompton.

KITTY. What were you – George, can you hear me?

GEORGE. I'm standing right here, Kitty.

KITTY. No, George, you're *not* standing, that's the – oh God. What *happened?*

JOSIAH. I can't say.

KITTY. Oh but you best start talking, Josiah –

GEORGE. I spoke my mind, Wild Cat.

KITTY. Georgie…

GEORGE. I got a right to –

KITTY. No, you've got no right doing that, because you don't give a boot about politics – the *moon*, that's what you talk about – the moon.

(**HANNAH** *is there with the water.*)

HANNAH. How many were there?

JOSIAH. A crowd of them, standing around him out front of –

KITTY. You *stood* there while –

JOSIAH. I was inside, arguing with McGreevy for cheating me on the seed like he did, when they dragged George out of the back room, already bleeding, saying this should be settled by single combat, George and this man Gibson.

KITTY. Gibson.

JOSIAH. But George was already bleeding powerful from the head, could hardly stand – and he tried to stand, Kitty – and that's when they decided he had *suffered enough.* That's what they said.

KITTY. Man named Gibson.

GEORGE. Murdered me like cowards.

KITTY. You never mind them now.

HANNAH. Here.

(**KITTY** *takes the wet cloth from* **HANNAH**.)

KITTY. Say something Christian over him.

HANNAH. May they burn in the devil's unquenchable fire.

(**HANNAH** *looks up at* **JOSIAH**.)

Every last one of them.

(**HANNAH** *and* **JOSIAH** *see that there is nothing more they can do.* **KITTY** *holds the cloth to* **GEORGE**'s *head. She sees there is nothing more she can do. She smiles down at him.*)

KITTY. Hey. Come on, George. Look at me. It's just me. We can do this. Together. See? All you got to do is love me. Leave *Kansas* out of it. Leave it all alone. Just – love me. George.

(**GEORGE** *dies.*)

Oh, George… Don't you leave me here.

(From far off, the sound of a whoop and a blazing fire. Blackout.)

End of Act I

ACT II

Interlude: Between God and Man

(HANNAH opens the door of the Clarke's cabin. There is a Sharps rifle standing there. She looks around. Picks it up. She speaks, loud enough to be overheard.)

HANNAH. Dear God. You must have heard my abolitionist prayer. Because here I find the very instrument of conversion I've been seeking, right outside this door.

(She holds the gun, feeling its weight.)

Beecher's Bible. Of my very own.

(A leather bag of bullets lands at her feet. **RED** *has tossed it.* **HANNAH** *locks eyes with him. They aren't playing.)*

RED. You'll be needing that.

HANNAH. You would know.

RED. Never said I didn't want a good fight, Boston.

HANNAH. What happened in Lawrence – what happened in *Lecompton* – is no good fight.

*(**HANNAH** loads the gun with an expertise we didn't think she had.)*

See what a girl can learn once she throws aside her needlework?

(She raises the rifle, takes her aim.)

I'm counting three, Ruffian, and then you best be out of range.

*(**RED** is gone.)*

*(**KITTY** stands in a field.)*

KITTY. Dear George.

(**GEORGE** *enters from the opposite direction, still in his bloodied clothes.*)

KITTY. *(cont.)* So. This is Kansas. Not that I'm complaining.

(The two see one another, across space and time.)

See, I was just wondering, George. What it is I am going to do now?

(They walk towards each other.)

Here in Kansas territory. Without you, standing right here. Without you lying there at my back. Without you set down across that table that never could stand straight, because George, you never were much of a carpenter.

(**GEORGE** *takes off his boots and places them on the mount of dirt at* **KITTY**'s *feet. He stands before her for the last time ever as* **GEORGE**.)

Not that I ever wanted a carpenter. Just your calloused hands. You. George.

(He continues on, and she talks to the grave at her feet.)

Is that Kansas soil resting easy on your bones?

(Elsewhere in space and time, he pulls on the boots of a different man.)

Are you resting easy under there while I'm – because I was wondering how it is you could leave me here, George, when I was set on following you to the dead end of this earth. I was just wondering: What am I going to do now? What can I do?

(He puts a long coat over his bloody shirt. He is now **JOHN BROWN**.*)*

JOHN BROWN. *(played by* **GEORGE**) I have no choice.

KITTY. Thought I'd start working on finishing up that fence. Pick up where you left off, over on the southern side the claim. But that's just something to wear myself out, as I'm looking over to the horizon.

JOHN BROWN. It has been ordained by the Almighty God, ordained from eternity...

KITTY. To that next farm over.

JOHN BROWN. That I should make an example of these men.

(He checks his bowie knife, his saber.)

KITTY. Be thinking on the *neighbors* we got here in Kansas, the ones still walking on this land while you lie underneath it.

JOHN BROWN. I've got only a short time to live –

KITTY. All them southern men.

JOHN BROWN. Only one death to die.

KITTY. Thinking what I'd like to do to them.

JOHN BROWN. And I will die fighting for this cause.

KITTY. What I would do.

JOHN BROWN. There will be no more peace in this land until slavery is done for!

*(**JOHN BROWN** raises his rifle over his head.)*

KITTY. Were I a *man* here in Kansas.

JOHN BROWN. If my name isn't John Brown.

*(**KITTY** picks up **GEORGE**'s boots and walks away from his grave. **JOHN BROWN** exits with a purpose in the opposite direction.)*

Scene Ten: A Bloody Place to Be

(**KITTY** *is drinking her morning coffee.* **HANNAH** *cleans her gun, bullets on the table.*)

KITTY. Got to fence off your claim, soon as you get to Kansas. That's what he told us, and now that's what I'm doing. Otherwise what's the difference between our lands? We drink the same whiskey, plow the same fields –

HANNAH. The difference is North and South – *this* land is Free Soil and –

KITTY. And there's nothing separatin' it from Josiah's, save the fence posts.

HANNAH. Those posts aren't going to *do* anything.

KITTY. It's a *line*, dividing us.

HANNAH. And, Kitty, your hands…

KITTY. What's the matter, afraid of a little red?

(**KITTY** *holds out her bloodied hands. She tosses* **HANNAH** *a fresh bandage.*)

I can't do it myself, Hannah Rose.

(**HANNAH** *puts down the rifle and begins wrapping* **KITTY**'s *hands.*)

I don't need to be workin' on that fence any more than you need to be cleanin' that rifle.

HANNAH. Gives me something to do.

KITTY. That Beecher's Bible's clean enough to sip tea in your sister's parlor.

HANNAH. What else can I do? There ain't an abolitionist press left standing in Kansas, and no one's gonna get caught carrying letters to the ones back East. This makes me feel –

KITTY. The same way I do, driving those posts into this Kansas land.

HANNAH. George is gone – *no one* has answered for that. We have to do *something*.

KITTY. My hands might be bloody, but they pale next to my thoughts. And I got nothin' else to carry me through these hot days, these long nights. Not my George, not my Flora – just a stake of land that somebody thought we could farm, and my *bloody thoughts.*

HANNAH. You got me, standin' beside you. This fight belongs to both of us now, Kitty, and I know that I am not your old man, but I will stand beside you, holding my –

KITTY. Bible? Just as long as you ain't talkin' about the good book.

*(**KITTY** leaves. **HANNAH** picks up the farmer's hat that **KITTY** forgot.)*

*(After a moment the door re-opens and **HANNAH** holds out the hat. But it is **RED**, who quickly closes the door behind him. She reaches for her gun, and he motions to the table.)*

RED. Lucky for me you got sense enough to remove the bullets.

(He finishes the coffee left in both cups. She puts down the useless gun.)

HANNAH. We haven't got any food.

RED. Didn't come here for food.

HANNAH. We haven't got any –

RED. You women *always* got something.

*(**HANNAH** holds her ground. **RED** circles her.)*

But I ain't sniffin' out that either, though I do notice yer lack of protest. You're lookin' different, Boston. More Kansas.

HANNAH. Here in this cabin, you're looking less Ruffian yourself.

RED. Then you're readin' me wrong.

HANNAH. If Kitty finds you –

RED. She's halfway to the southern side of the claim, just like yesterday and the day before – and yes, I have been watchin' out, this time for my own hide. I've got *news* for you. I know you must be hungry for it, with no man bringin' it home. What's goin' 'round the whiskey barrel in town.

*(She holds tight to **KITTY**'s hat, restraining herself.)*

HANNAH. The *news*. Red.

RED. Man named John Brown.

HANNAH. Never heard of him.

RED. No one did, three days ago. But him and a couple of his kinfolk have created quite an impression. Callin' it the Pottawatomie Massacre – bloody, bloody work – how they came upon these farmers, middle of the night, asleep in their beds with their wives.

Dragged 'em a short ways from their cabins – one together with his sons, stabbed 'em clear through the chest. Sliced open another one's head, knife wounds to his face and sides. The fingers and arms of the youngest one cut up and cut off, because he must have been holdin' up his hands, tryin' to protect his face. Say John Brown watched the whole thing as if in a trance – then put a bullet in a man's forehead.

HANNAH. You tryin' to scare me off – show me how lowdown you Ruffians are? Is this your kind of a *warning*, Red?

RED. A warning – ?

HANNAH. Middle of the night, if John Brown shows up at my door –

RED. Show 'em your worn-out copy of *Uncle Tom's*. He's an abolitionist, don't you know. "Holy Warrior," he calls himself.

HANNAH. John Brown?

RED. Didn't think you had it in you, you Christians.

HANNAH. Well, then –

RED. Neither did you, from that look.

HANNAH. I guess you're wrong there.

RED. See Boston, this is my kind of a *good-bye*. This fight is upon us – don't you know, Kansas is a bloody place to be. Would have put it all down on paper, but that ain't safe. *These* ain't.

(**RED** *holds out a packet of several letters, written to him by* **HANNAH**.)

Wouldn't want to get caught with your hand on my person.

HANNAH. You could've burned 'em.

RED. I'd be lyin' if I said I didn't try. Thought to put 'em in the ground too, but a man can only dig so deep with bare hands. I might be a Ruffian, but I like to give mine better than a shallow grave.

HANNAH. Thank you for returning them.

(*She takes the letters from him.* **RED** *stands close enough to smell* **HANNAH**'s *sweat. He takes* **KITTY**'s *hat from her hand and puts it on, pulls it low.*)

RED. I can't be caught stealin' from this cabin near dawn, any more than an abolitionist can be caught alive in Lecompton. You got the news. Now you steer clear of town.

HANNAH. John Brown. Where's he now?

RED. Keepin' to the woods by day, movin' along the roads by darkness. Knockin' on doors in the dead of night – or not knockin' at all – *both* sides now, bringing terror to this Kansas land.

HANNAH. If they come –

RED. You better pray we don't.

HANNAH. You better watch yourself, Red. And that *is* a warning.

RED. Don't count on seein' *myself* any time soon. Any luck I'll be back at McGreevy's with my powerful thirst.

HANNAH. What kinda Ruffian does that make you?

RED. One still standin' in his boots. I *seen* what we done, Boston. You best bolt this door.

(**RED** *leaves.*)

Scene Eleven: The Dead of Night

(**HANNAH** *holds on to her gun.*)

HANNAH. Dear Abigail. We sleep with our guns now. I sleep with a *gun*, Abby. And though I spend the daytime in full confidence of my aim and shot, in the dead of night, I turn to prayer.

But if God is hearing my prayer – is he also hearing Louisa's, asking him to keep away the bloody abolitionists? And what does God do with these two prayers, put together with the prayer of John Brown and of Kitty – because I know her lips are moving for something even if she doesn't call it that.

And my prayer isn't anything like the ones we were taught as girls. It is full of vengeance and self-preservation and a powerful need, to hold on to *something* – while we wait in darkness, as our moment of reckoning comes closer and closer and closer and –

(**KITTY** *stands at the window.*)

KITTY. Torches. Coming down the road.

HANNAH. Stand back from the –

KITTY. Can't see me from there, and so what if they do?

HANNAH. Which side?

KITTY. We all look the same now, doll. But I think you know which one I'm powerful ready for.

HANNAH. Here, help me push the table in front of the door.

KITTY. If they want in, they'll have their way – no table's gonna –

HANNAH. It'll slow them down. We don't have a bolt, Kitty.

(*Together they move the table against the door.*)

HANNAH. How many are there?

KITTY. Two carrying torches, but I'd count on more than that.

HANNAH. Kitty, I'm –

KITTY. I don't want to hear it, unless it's how you're fully prepared to –

HANNAH. I am – this is why I came to Kansas –

KITTY. This is for *George*.

HANNAH. But all the talking and writing and waiting – none of it changes my shaking hands.

KITTY. Long as you can aim that rifle. Don't think these Southern men will just turn away when we don't have a man to turn over to them.

HANNAH. I know that.

KITTY. Each one of 'em's heard what John Brown did. They've got somethin' to settle –

HANNAH. So do we.

*(**KITTY** checks the window.)*

KITTY. They've left the road –

HANNAH. Coming – ?

KITTY. This way.

HANNAH. I've said prayers –

KITTY. Me too – just in case.

HANNAH. But, Kitty, I don't know if –

*(Knocking at the door. **KITTY** answers with a sure voice.)*

KITTY. Who's there?

FIRST MAN. *(played by **GEORGE**)* Are you with the Free Soil party?

*(**KITTY** looks to **HANNAH**.)*

KITTY. We are.

SECOND MAN. *(played by **RED**)* Who's there?

HANNAH. Two of us.

*(**THIRD MAN** tries to open the door, stopped by the table.)*

FIRST MAN. Kindly unbolt the door.

*(**KITTY** holds her rifle ready and nods to **HANNAH**, who moves the table. **FIRST MAN** and **SECOND MAN** enter. **THIRD MAN** stands just outside the door.)*

SECOND MAN. It's only the *two* of you – here in this whole cabin?

KITTY. My old man's dead.

FIRST MAN. Free Soil, was he?

KITTY. And died for it, so I got nothin' left to loose.

THIRD MAN. *(played by* **JOSIAH***)* Except yer hide.

SECOND MAN. And how do we know you're not lyin' –

HANNAH. My Harriet Beecher Stowe.

(**HANNAH** *hands the book that she's been holding to* **FIRST MAN**.)

Abolitionist.

KITTY. Are you Southern gentlemen?

SECOND MAN. And if we are?

KITTY. I will *have* your blood on my hands!

(**FIRST MAN** *motions to* **SECOND MAN** *to lower his gun.*)

FIRST MAN. We believe in John Brown's cause. Have you heard news of John Brown?

HANNAH. We have.

(**HANNAH** *breathes relief, but* **KITTY** *still holds her gun.*)

KITTY. How do we know –

SECOND MAN. This meetin' wouldn't be half so cordial.

FIRST MAN. You'll have to excuse us. We're from south of Lawrence – not familiar with these parts. This close to Lecompton, a man can't be sure which side the cabins're on.

(**KITTY** *lowers her gun.* **FIRST MAN** *hands the book back to* **HANNAH**.)

KITTY. Free Soil. Like I said.

FIRST MAN. Then we'll proceed to town.

(**FIRST MAN** *and* **SECOND MAN** *head for the door.*)

KITTY. But my neighbor ain't.

(This stops them.)

SECOND MAN. Which one's that?

KITTY. Next farm over's Josiah Nichols' place. From Missouri, he is.

FIRST MAN. Many thanks, ladies.

THIRD MAN. I'll git th'boys.

*(They leave, and **KITTY** goes to the window.)*

HANNAH. This will be my last letter to you, Abby – for some time. But I don't want you to be alarmed – I know you must have other concerns, what with little James… Remember to give my nephew a kiss from me. Tell him where I've gone.

I can't say when I'll be returning to Boston. What with the distance between that place – between *any* other place – and Kansas – that long lonely road – I really can't say. And after what I've seen here –

(She stops herself. Writes something different.)

Kansas – *blooming* like it is. Wild flowers, as far as the eyes can reach. Makes me think: Why is it you all work so hard cultivating flowers in New England? When the real reward is watching the landscape explode, with that vibrant – all that *red*.

Scene Twelve: Taking Leave

(Just before sunrise, **JOSIAH** *stands in the doorway, barefoot and covered with soot.* **KITTY** *has the Indian blanket wrapped around her.* **HANNAH** *holds her rifle.)*

JOSIAH. Don't need that rifle, miss. We're good as gone.

KITTY. Hannah, go warm the coffee.

JOSIAH. Didn't come here for coffee.

KITTY. Well, I'm afraid we don't have anything stronger –

JOSIAH. Don't want your – I think you can see, my eyes have red enough.

KITTY. Then I guess this is a good-bye. Hannah. The coffee.

*(***HANNAH*** goes to warm the coffee.)*

JOSIAH. We came here for the same reasons you did. Me and Louisa. To farm and to have our family, and make it easier for the young ones to one day scrape together a living than it was for us.

KITTY. We came from different places –

JOSIAH. But we wanted the *same* things –

KITTY. Two *different* things, just happen to be mixing and mingling together in one pot.

JOSIAH. Me and George, all we wanted was to be able to live *our* lives in our *own way* –

KITTY. And there was a *difference* in those ways, and my George died for that difference, and you'd be lyin' to say otherwise, Josiah Nichols – this here is Kansas Territory. And Kansas ain't Missouri.

JOSIAH. It's *America.*

KITTY. And what's that supposed to mean? Because I lack the *confidence* in that word.

JOSIAH. I know I got rights, Kitty. That's my belief, and I know it in my heart. And I know it ain't right, what they're doing here in Kansas. Because I been working this land, and that gives me certain rights to live here as a Southern man. This is our America, and we got a right to it. It's only *right.*

KITTY. Like your right to kill my old man?

JOSIAH. I carried him home to you.

KITTY. You were his *neighbor* – you sat here at our table drinking whiskey – how could you let them do that to him?

JOSIAH. Wasn't nothing more I could do.

KITTY. You can do *everything*, Josiah. From that window there I watched you build that cabin out of nothing – all you had to do was look at that land and it was ready to yield up its crops to you. So don't tell me –

JOSIAH. I was too late! I thought he was just some dumb Yankee there in Lecompton the day that Lawrence was being sacked. By the time I saw it was George, he was inside a circle of men, all of them drunk and with knives – I was too late. And when I picked him up off the ground – as gentle as I would my own wife – he was already bleeding his life away, he was, George – right into the wood of my wagon.

KITTY. Well, I hope they burned that wagon with the rest of it. Because that's just not good enough, I'm sorry, Josiah, but that just won't do.

JOSIAH. I'm sorry –

KITTY. Those were *your* people who did that, you *are* what you *are* –

JOSIAH. But I came for his boots.

*(**HANNAH** is standing there with the coffee pot. She hands **KITTY** and **JOSIAH** cups, pours the thick dark liquid.)*

I know you got them, so don't stand there like you don't. I watched you bury him from our window. Louisa wanted to go to you. She was asking me to hold the baby so that she could – but I wouldn't hear her words, just stood there – for the first time in my life standing idle – hearing that colicky child cry, watching you across that field that seemed to have grown wider in a day. With the sun going down, I could make out a woman standing on the horizon, holding a pair of boots.

*(**KITTY** sips her coffee.)*

JOSIAH. *(cont.)* I need those boots, missus. Yes, they burned my wagon with the rest of it. And now I'm walking to Missouri, and I ain't got nothing for my feet.

KITTY. They came here first, you know. Didn't know which cabin's which. Hannah had to show 'em her book for proof – didn't you, doll? One look at me, they knew I'd lost everything already, wouldn't be bothered lying to save my own life. But *your* life, neighbor. Your farm. I could have lied to save that. And I didn't.

JOSIAH. You told them I was –

KITTY. From Missouri. Proslavery. That's what you *are*. I gave that information freely.

JOSIAH. Did you.

(**JOSIAH** *takes a sip from his cup. His hand, for the first time in his life, shaking.*)

Well, then. They did find their way. Came up quietly – lying there in our beds, we didn't know it until they were forcing open the door, looking around the cabin and helping themselves with a clear conscience since they knew what would happen to it all otherwise.

One of 'em takes his hand, sticks it in the honey pot that Louisa had filled just that morning – he's licking my wife's honey off his dirty fingers, not even looking me in the eye. Not hearing the young 'ins cry, or maybe just not paying them any mind – maybe he's got a colicky child at home himself.

And the other cowards're out back, setting fire to my home. Setting my fields to fire – my first crop – and all I can think is: Why'd they have to burn the crop? Can you tell me why they had to do that, Kittson?

KITTY. I don't know.

JOSIAH. Burnin' it just as it's beginning to grow, when they *know* I am not going to be here for the harvest. Now, see –

(**JOSIAH** *pours the hot coffee onto his feet.*)

JOSIAH. *(cont.)* My feet are hard.

(He holds out his hand to them.)

Calloused, same as my hands. Don't make me make them bloody.

*(****KITTY*** *doesn't flinch.* ***HANNAH*** *gets the boots.)*

HANNAH. The boots are here. They're yours, Josiah. I'm giving them – Kitty, you can't stop me – I know they're not mine to give, but I'm giving them to you anyway. The ax is out back, if you need to open the toes, George –

KITTY. Had small feet, for a man of his size.

*(****HANNAH*** *places the boots in front of* ***JOSIAH****.)*

JOSIAH. Then. I best be going. The youngins.

(He picks up the boots. ***KITTY*** *takes the Indian blanket off her back and offers it to him.)*

KITTY. For Louisa. She can wrap her little one in this. That's what I was going to do.

JOSIAH. Louisa didn't make it out. Makin' sure everyone else did. But if she had, I know she would have appreciated that.

*(****JOSIAH*** *exits with the boots, leaving the blanket.)*

HANNAH. I watched you watch it burn. When I looked over at you, saw your eyes out the window. And if you were looking anywhere *near* that window, you could see nothing but –

KITTY. My mind was someplace else.

HANNAH. Don't tell me about your – I want to know what it felt like. Lying there on your side, unable to turn your eyes from –

KITTY. Didn't feel like I thought. That's what you want to hear, isn't it? Well, it felt nothing like a fever breaking. It was the end of *nothing*.

HANNAH. Then – why, Kitty?

KITTY. I had no choice.

HANNAH. What good was it?

KITTY. What was I supposed to do, after they killed my George?

HANNAH. They – Josiah and Louisa – did not kill –

KITTY. It was their people, it was *them*. And you yourself said they should burn in hell, every last one. You said that as plain as I'm standing here –

HANNAH. I did say that. I believed in it then.

KITTY. And what is it you believe now?

HANNAH. I believe – I *know* – that slavery is a sin against man and nation and –

KITTY. How far will you go? For that belief of yours – once you put aside your *letters* – because tonight you just stood there, while I filled up that doorframe. It was *me* who sent those men with torches on down the road.

HANNAH. It was *wrong*, Kitty. What happened here tonight was –

KITTY. You saw the torches, you knew exactly what was going to happen when they got to that next farm, and you stood there and let it happen, so now don't tell me it was –

HANNAH. Wrong as your old man's boots walking to Missouri. And I know that I let it happen. *Prayed* for something like that to happen, and now that's what I need to stake out. My head and my heart and my country...

(**HANNAH** *collects her books, one by one, putting them in her sack.*)

All this wrong being done in the name of God.

KITTY. You know, Hannah Rose, we might both be women, but our blood is not the same flavor. I'm a wild cat. He always said. So don't you go holdin' your books over me.

HANNAH. I'm not. I'm taking them with me.

(**HANNAH** *opens the door on the dawn.*)

KITTY. What makes you think you can survive two bits outside that door?

HANNAH. Nothing. But when you got nothing but *your life* to give – what's there to fear in Kansas?

(**HANNAH** *walks out the door.*)

Scene Thirteen: Lecompton, the Wildest and Wickedest Town

(The back room of McCreevy's store. Three Border Ruffians who crossed over, never went home. Too busy drinking. Too much whooping and looting and fighting going on.)

MAN STINKIN'. *(played by* **GEORGE***)* Abolitionizin'. Here abolitionizin' all over this Southern territory. Stickin' their Bibles 'n' rifles 'n' all other sorts of instruments of abolitionizin' in all kinds of places that nature never intended.

RED. Strange breed.

MAN DRINKIN'. *(played by* **JOSIAH***)* White-livered.

MAN STINKIN'. Ever cut one open? Liver's white. Bright white. With negro-lovin' spots all over it.

MAN DRINKIN'. Chicken-hearted.

MAN STINKIN'. You ever smell one?

RED. A live one?

MAN STINKIN'. W'all smell the same dead, Red.

RED. That so.

MAN STINKIN'. So, yes, I'm sayin' a live one. Squirms under yer thumb. One live abolitionist.

MAN DRINKIN'. Catch 'em by the toe.

MAN STINKIN'. Smellin' like that *particular* Yankee soap they all use. I'd swear they pass it around, one single cake of it, cabin-a-cabin – wash their wives in between the sheets, and then pony express it to the next. Press it into the palms of all them impressionable farmers they converted with their slicked-up Bibles –

RED. Blue-bellies.

MAN DRINKIN'. All of 'em.

MAN STINKIN'. Each one not from Missouri.

RED. Yankees.

MAN STINKIN'. So you smelled that smell?

RED. I've smelled the burning cabins. On both sides the road.

MAN DRINKIN'. Not that smell.

MAN STINKIN'. Shoot, that burn was because they wouldn't come out 'n' fight. But I am referrin' to that burn you feel when you're standin' outside McGreevy's and you see 'em walk through this town, like this land was free – some kinda *free country*. Like they got any right to be here, settin' up them farms, when we're here –

RED. Drinkin' the red eye.

MAN STINKIN'. That's right.

MAN DRINKIN'. Cussin'.

(**MAN STINKIN'** *spits on the floor.*)

MAN DRINKIN'. Spittin'.

MAN STINKIN'. And don't forget all the *whorin'* we're gonna be doin' jist as soon as we git us some whores here in Kansas Territory. Generally doing what nature intended us.

RED. That right, *Morris*?

MAN STINKIN'. It's Mo. As in –

MAN DRINKIN'. Low Mo.

MAN STINKIN'. And jist so you know, Low Mo don't appreciate no one steppin' on his –

MAN DRINKIN'. Boots. Like you been doin' here all day.

MAN STINKIN'. I was sayin' 'bout that Yankee smell. Which you ain't smelled for yerself.

MAN DRINKIN'. Have you, Red?

RED. W'all stink the same dead.

(**RED** *smells trouble. He's on his guard.*)

MAN STINKIN'. But I'm talkin' that moment right before dead – you got 'em close, smell the fear mixin' and minglin' with the Yankee soap – like you surprised them in the middle of their washin', dropped the soap right there on th' ground. Dirt adherin' to it. Jist like yer boots.

RED. What about my boots?

MAN STINKIN'. I'm talkin' 'bout *you*, Red. What we heard 'round McGreevy's. And jist so you know –

MAN DRINKIN'. Mo's boots 'r' small.

MAN STINKIN'. Pinch my feet, 'specially in this heat.

MAN DRINKIN'. Red's feet 'r' big.

MAN STINKIN'. You ain't smelled the smell of Yankee fear. Have ya.

RED. Who's sayin'?

MAN STINKIN'. Got a taste for that –

MAN DRINKIN'. Yankee pie.

MAN STINKIN'. What kinda Ruffian are ya, Red?

RED. I expect you've heard plenty 'bout Edwin Redpath.

MAN DRINKIN'. Abolitionizin' sympathizin'.

MAN STINKIN'. That's what we heard.

RED. Nothin' simpatico about me.

MAN DRINKIN'. Shoot.

*(**STINKIN'** draws his bowie knife, looks how it shines.)*

MAN STINKIN'. Round these parts, got to be *sure* where a man stands.

MAN DRINKIN'. Or lies.

MAN STINKIN'. So we gonna settle this now, Red, let me tell you how: I bet yer *boots* that you can't scalp an abolitionist before the sun sets.

RED. Little late in the day to be makin' such a wager.

MAN STINKIN'. What's the matter – you *yellow*, Red?

*(The men laugh. **STINKIN'** holds his bowie, standing in between **RED** and the door.)*

RED. What's in it for me?

MAN STINKIN'. Bring us that Yankee scalp, and we'll let you walk upright out of McGreevy's – no mo' questions asked – walk out of this here town of Lecompton, all the way back to Missouri. Now. We simpatico on that?

(breathing)

RED. I heard.

MAN DRINKIN'. I'll watch yer red eye.

MAN STINKIN'. Oh, he'll *need* his red eye.

MAN DRINKIN'. All afternoon you been lookin' at his boots –

MAN STINKIN'. Shoot.

MAN DRINKIN'. But I been *waitin'* on his whiskey!

MAN STINKIN'. Have you, Seymour?

*(**MAN DRINKIN'** and **MAN STINKIN'** face it off. Hot whiskey breath.)*

RED. This whiskey ain't my whiskey no more.

*(**RED** sends his jug sliding across the table. Without moving his eyes, **MAN DRINKIN'** grabs it before it goes over.)*

MAN DRINKIN'. Can't take it with ya.

*(**DRINKIN'** exits with the jug.)*

MAN STINKIN'. Don't hold yer breath, Red. That moment, before yer abolitionist drops like just another stinkin' body. Don't forget to breathe.

*(**MAN DRINKIN'** pushes **HANNAH** into the room.)*

MAN DRINKIN'. There he is.

MAN STINKIN'. Sorry to keep you waitin', miss.

*(As he passes by, **MAN STINKIN'** gives **HANNAH** a little sniff.)*

MAN STINKIN'. Pretty pigtails ya got there.

(He leaves, whooping.)

Scene Fourteen: North Meets South, Again

*(**RED** and **HANNAH**, alone together in back of McGreevy's store. She is empty-handed, looking worse for the wear.)*

RED. You should not be here. I don't know what those two Ruffians done tol' you, but –

HANNAH. They said I could find you here.

RED. Back rooms are *back* rooms for a reason, Boston.

HANNAH. I was looking for you, I asked McGreevy –

RED. You should not have *done* that –

HANNAH. He cussed at me.

RED. You should never have come here. *Kansas.*

*(**RED** spits on the floor.)*

HANNAH. I had a powerful belief in that word. Until I just let it go, along with everything else I was holding on to. Sent my books floating on down the river – I imagined they'd float. Especially the Bible. Ever see the word of God sinking before your eyes, Red?

RED. Every day.

HANNAH. Their pages soaking up the Kansas River with a thirst you never thought existed between those tightly bound covers, all laced up – coming undone, heavy with the Kansas, sinking lower and lower, spread out like Ophelia's skirts – down to the gravel bottom, scratching out their words. Drowned them all.

RED. Shoulda sold 'em, leather hides –

HANNAH. No one's got any use for books in Kansas. Not even kindling, in this heat.

RED. Where's yer Beecher's Bible? Use that 'bout now. Fire away at every Southern man within range.

HANNAH. I'm not going to do that.

RED. So you've given up yer abolitionizin' ways –

HANNAH. I ain't saying that either, but the fight I seen here in Kansas's two parts terror, one part blood – not quite what *abolitionist* means to me. And that's not what I'm here for now. I think you know.

RED. Haven't got any more whiskey.

HANNAH. Neither do I.

RED. And I think you know that's all I'm good for, miss. Nothing here but a man and his boots. Bowie knife down one side, another on his belt.

HANNAH. I want something else.

(His hand inching towards his bowie.)

RED. What did you think you were gonna get here? Back of McGreevy's – I'm a Ruffian, and I got one thing for you –

HANNAH. The territory of the line.

RED. And that ain't it.

(His hand holds on the knife.)

HANNAH. The line itself. That's where I want to go. You and me, together. A place where it's not one side or another, not you being one thing and me being another. Some place where the land is just land – and no one's staked a claim. Let's go there.

*(**HANNAH** stands close enough to touch him. She does. **RED** can't draw his knife. He can't look away either.)*

RED. No such place.

HANNAH. What if there was?

RED. There ain't and I know it, because my boots are stuck in this soil and it's *red*, like my blood and your blood – that's what's in between Boston and Kansas.

HANNAH. I'm not talking about Kansas. Leave *Kansas* out of it.

RED. It's where we're standing.

HANNAH. I mean some place that's just –

RED. What?

HANNAH. America.

RED. Two sides to *America* – North and South, no matter how far west you go, and they meet right here. Nice to meet you. They call me Red. See this is me introducin' myself proper, Boston.

HANNAH. Don't call me that. That's not who I am anymore –

RED. Don't have much of a choice.

HANNAH. That's not who you are, either.

RED. I got a wager against a pair of boots says it's so.

HANNAH. And what is it you're betting on?

RED. The scalp of an abolitionist.

HANNAH. Well, then.

RED. Yours.

(She doesn't flinch. They stare each other down.)

HANNAH. That's something that you haven't got. You're going to have to *get* that, Red.

RED. Are you picking a fight with me, miss?

HANNAH. I'm saying what's true.

RED. Because this is no game, I'm not bluffing –

HANNAH. True as the boots on your feet.

RED. And these men – Boston, you don't know –

HANNAH. I been in Kansas as long as you have.

RED. These men –

HANNAH. Will kill you.

RED. Because they've got nothin' else to do.

HANNAH. I know that. But I also know you. And I don't think you'll do it.

RED. I'm a Ruffian.

HANNAH. You're just a man.

RED. Whoop louder, jump higher, get drunker –

HANNAH. Edwin Redpath, I *know* you.

RED. Then you'll understand what I'm going to have to do.

HANNAH. You still haven't done it.

RED. Because as usual, you won't shut yer mouth!

HANNAH. Look, you're shaking in –

RED. You don't know a thing about what I am inside these boots.

HANNAH. I am imagining how you feel.

RED. You can't do that, schoolteacher.

HANNAH. Yes, I can. That's what we all need to do.

RED. We need to know what we *are*. That never changes – that's all we need to know.

HANNAH. There ain't so much separating us. A thin wire of mistrust, which I am about to step over and walk out of here, with each and every hair on my –

RED. There's nowhere to go! This is as *far* as you go.

(**RED** *draws his bowie knife, holding it in between* **HANNAH** *and the door.*)

RED. Why'd you have to come here?

HANNAH. Because I had a powerful need.

RED. You can't walk away from this.

HANNAH. Watch me. You're gonna watch me as I walk through that –

(**RED** *grabs* **HANNAH**. *He stands behind her, knife drawn, and for a moment we don't know what's to happen. Then he begins to smell her hair. He moves around to the front of her body, and smells up to her neck. This is dangerous and strange and the closest they will ever get. They look one another in the eyes, one last breath. He moves away.*)

RED. This is not over.

HANNAH. It is for me.

RED. I am letting you go. Not thinkin' on you, not writing you no more letters. I'm not watching out for you either – got no more whiskey, don't even know what shape that drop is. But don't for a *second* turn your back thinkin' this fight is over. Not for a single one of us in this land.

HANNAH. This land is tired. *Kansas* is tired. When's the last time you turned your face out three feet past McGreevy's door? The people have seen the red, Red, and now they're just staring back empty.

RED. This country's still divided.

HANNAH. I guess we are. But America's not really what I was searching for today. I'd be lying if I said something closer wasn't on my mind.

RED. Go home, Hannah Rose.

HANNAH. I will, Edwin. Soon as I find where that is.

*(**HANNAH** walks out. **RED** watches her go. He lowers himself, holding on to his boots.)*

Scene Fifteen: At the End of the Day

(**KITTY** *stands outside her cabin.* **HANNAH** *approaches.*)

KITTY. Thought you might be turning up today. Had a feeling. I had a powerful dream last night, after a night of fitful slumber. I was in the middle of a field.

HANNAH. Kansas field?

KITTY. No, it was just a field, somewhere under the sky – not *God*'s sky, just sky.

HANNAH. I wasn't going to say God.

KITTY. I just – thought you might.

(**KITTY** *holds on to the toy horse as she tells her dream.*)

In my dream, there was a powerful bright sun, and I squinted right into it. And it was only then – when I was looking just where I shouldn't have been – that I saw her. My little girl, I lost along the way.

HANNAH. Flora.

KITTY. Just this tiny shape on the horizon, but then as she got closer I could see that she was a girl, and then that she was *my girl*. Come back to me. And I was flooded with joy, like the Kansas River washing over me all at once, a flood like haven't felt in – some time. Not since –

HANNAH. George.

KITTY. So she starts to run towards me, her voice squealing in my ears – so reckless and with those wildflowers up to her waist, I thought sure she'd tumble right over. But she didn't. Not until she got right up to my legs and fell into *me*, laughing, grabbing hold so I couldn't take a step.

(**KITTY** *digs a hole in the dirt near* **GEORGE***'s grave, and buries the child's toy.*)

KITTY. We held it like that for what felt like a year in the sun, but maybe was just a few moments of breathing. And then she let me go. Slipped away, when I glanced up at the horizon. Or maybe she grew right into my legs, becoming a part of me again, helping me to stand.

(**KITTY** *wipes the dirt from her hands.*)

HANNAH. That dream means you're whole.

KITTY. Then it would be lying. Not yet, anyway. Something I need.

(She takes out paper and pencil.)

A letter.

HANNAH. I'm not doing that anymore –

KITTY. Not for *you*, doll –

HANNAH. I got nothin' left to –

KITTY. This one's for *me*. Can't write the words to save my life, any more than I could read the Bible, and so you're gonna do this for me. Because I got a powerful need.

(**KITTY** *sets the paper and pencil down in front of* **HANNAH.***)*

To address a man named Gibson.

(**HANNAH** *takes up the pencil.*)

HANNAH. Dear Mr. Gibson.

KITTY. Dear Mr. Gibson. You do not know me. And I believe you never knew my husband George. But I have heard tell that he died by your hand. Or maybe you were only part of a crowd, but I account you just the same. When you dealt him blows, I imagine…

(**KITTY** *imagines it.*)

HANNAH. I imagine.

KITTY. I imagine – you never thought about the woman he had loving him. You saw a man who was unlike yourself. Who said things that were contrary to what you held to be true, about your God or your country, and inside that, you found reason to strike this man. Again and again and again, until he fell to the ground. Until he was bleeding his life into Kansas soil.

(She breathes.)

Are you with me?

HANNAH. I am.

(**KITTY** *continues more rapidly.*)

KITTY. And though you do not know me, I want you to remember this. I am not a man, but I can *fire a rifle* and if ever the time comes that we do meet, I will send you to a place – to a place of *eternal fire*.

(**HANNAH** *has stopped.*)

Write it, Hannah Rose – these words *need* to be written.

HANNAH. To a place…

KITTY. Of eternal fire.

HANNAH. Of weeping and gnashing of teeth.

(The women look at one another with a shared understanding.)

KITTY. Because I've got no belief for your God in heaven, but I have tasted the flavor of hell. And I would like to share it with you. Because whatever has befallen you this summer, you have not *suffered enough*.

(**KITTY** *spits into the dirt.* **HANNAH** *folds the letter and gives it to* **KITTY**.)

HANNAH. What are we going to do?

KITTY. Try again.

(**KITTY** *takes the letter and presses it into the dirt and spit. She folds it again, with mud inside of it, and puts it inside her dress, next to her heart.*)

HANNAH. We can't – after what's happened, what we've seen and done –

KITTY. That's what we *do*.

HANNAH. But – where?

KITTY. Right here. Kansas.

HANNAH. Kansas.

KITTY. Isn't that why people come to the Kansas Territory?

HANNAH. No one's going to come to Kansas anymore. Nothing here now but ruined towns, burnt farms, burnt Bibles, crops rotting in the fields –

KITTY. And a glorious patch of tobacco out back – this land is *rich*, doll. If I can make it grow with my two beans, then any farmer can. So they'll come. For the Kansas soil. And this land here – which has been *untouched* for some time – will begin to remember, what that feels like.

*(**KITTY** lights her pipe. The women pass it back and forth, smoking it together.)*

HANNAH. We're not going to forget.

KITTY. We'll carry it on our chest, but we'll carry. We can do this, doll. Together. And at the end of a long day on the farm, in the schoolhouse…

HANNAH. At the end of a very *long* summer.

KITTY. We'll sit here, look up to the sky.

HANNAH. Not God's sky.

KITTY. Not Venice, Italy.

HANNAH. No Boston.

KITTY. No man's sky, but *ours*.

HANNAH. But you know this isn't over, Kitty.

KITTY. Kansas is just beginning.

HANNAH. I mean, in this country – North against South, neighbor against neighbor – it's not *over* –

KITTY. Just becoming a state, Kansas – free state, that is. And here I am, not even minding the snakes anymore. And they don't seem to be minding me either. I got to thinking about how they must feel, us moving in on their belly-stretching territory, and decided I'd just let them be to slither about the place.

Look, doll – would you look at that? Kansas sunset.

*(**KITTY** looks to the sky. **HANNAH** turns and looks, seeing something different.)*

HANNAH. Red.

KITTY. Enough to fill the whole window. That's something to write home about, Hannah Rose.

(**KITTY** *points to the remaining piece of paper in front of* **HANNAH**.*)*

This one's for yerself. So you don't forget. Write it with your feet planted right here, just outside your new home.

(**KITTY** *leaves her be.* **HANNAH** *looks at the empty page. Then she looks out at the land, all at once, seeing the past and imagining the future.)*

HANNAH. Dear Abigail. Much has happened here in Kansas. As evidenced by my hands being dirty. My eyes are red. I have much to write, about America. Abby, *this* is America.

End of Play

OTHER TITLES AVAILABLE FROM SAMUEL FRENCH

VICTORIA MARTIN: MATH TEAM QUEEN

Kathryn Walat

Comedy / 4m, 1f / Unit Set

When uber-popular Vickie Martin joins the all-male math team, chaos theory becomes the rule at Longwood High School. Can this goddess of Pi possibly make the mathletes victorious? Totally.

"The tale about overcoming odds is surprisingly touching."
– *Time Out New York*

"The biggest and best surprise of the season so far...puts the nerds next to the popular kids as they join forces to prove their worth to the world. Victoria Martin leaves audiences both laughing and cheering."
– *NYTheatre.com*

SAMUELFRENCH.COM

OTHER TITLES AVAILABLE FROM SAMUEL FRENCH

AMERICAN TALES

Book and Lyrics by Ken Stone
Music by Jan Powell

Musical in two acts, based on stories
by classic American writers

Musical in two acts, based on stories by classic American writers / 4m, 1f / Period costumes and set pieces, mid to late 19th century

**Ovation Award nomination for Best Book/Lyrics/Music
Kleban Award winner, Libretto *(Bartleby, the Scrivener)***

Act I, *The Loves of Alonzo Fitz Clarence and Rosannah Ethelton*, is from Mark Twain's story of two people falling in love at a great distance with the aid of that brand-new invention, the telephone. Alonzo in Maine and Rosannah in California meet by the accident of crossed wires and each falls in love with an imagined ideal of the other. So complete is their self-deception that even when brought face to face they cannot recognize each other. Love is found, lost, and found again. Played as period melodrama, but the relevance to 21st century dating habits is clear.

Act II, *Bartleby, the Scrivener*, is dramatized from Herman Melville's slyly funny but ultimately tragic story. Building on the theme of human connections made and missed, this act takes a darker turn, looking at people who occupy the closest of quarters and yet don't really communicate at all. Bartleby, employed as a copyist in a law office of the 1840s, inexplicably begins to refuse to work, forcing his colleagues to ask themselves the transforming question that ends the play: What do we owe to the people who come into our lives?

"Excellent new musical."
– Critic's Choice, *The Los Angeles Times*

OTHER TITLES AVAILABLE FROM SAMUEL FRENCH

DORIS TO DARLENE

Jordan Harrison

Comedy / 4m, 2f / Unit Set

Doris to Darlene, A Cautionary Valentine: In the candy-colored 1960s, biracial schoolgirl Doris is molded into pop star Darlene by a whiz-kid record producer who culls a top-ten hit out of Richard Wagner's "Liebestod." Rewind to the candy-colored 1860s, where Wagner is writing the melody that will become Darlene's hit song. Fast-forward to the not-so-candy-colored present, where a teenager obsesses over Darlene's music – and his music teacher. Three dissonant decades merge into an unlikely harmony in this time-jumping pop fairy tale about the dreams and disasters behind one transcendent song.

"*Doris to Darlene: A Cautionary Valentine* is a quirky and enjoyable love letter to music and its seductive power to make us lose ourselves…Harrison's language is by turns so punchy, poetic and observant."
– *New York Daily News*

"Mr. Harrison's play has an affectionate, music-loving heart."
– *The New York Times*

"*Doris to Darlene* has much going for it: Harrison's intelligence, originality and passion."
– *Time Out New York*

"Harrison's teasing, rapturous chamber opera of a play spins and crackles like a beloved old 78 under a bamboo needle…*Doris to Darlene* is that rare thing: a rarefied theatrical experiment that has the glow of pure entertainment and the warmth of a folktale."
– *Newsday*

SAMUELFRENCH.COM

OTHER TITLES AVAILABLE FROM SAMUEL FRENCH

THE WHIPPING MAN

Matthew Lopez

Drama / 3m / Interior

It is April, 1865. The Civil War is over and throughout the south, slaves are being freed, soldiers are returning home and in Jewish homes, the annual celebration of Passover is being celebrated. Into the chaos of war-torn Richmond comes Caleb DeLeon, a young Confederate officer who has been severely wounded. He finds his family's home in ruins and abandoned, save for two former slaves, Simon and John, who wait in the empty house for the family's return. As the three men wait for signs of life to return to the city, they wrestle with their shared past, the bitter irony of Jewish slave-owning and the reality of the new world in which they find themselves. The sun sets on the last night of Passover and Simon - having adopted the religion of his masters - prepares a humble Seder to observe the ancient celebration of the freeing of the Hebrew slaves from Egypt, noting with particular satisfaction the parallels to their current situation. But the pain of their enslavement will not be soothed by this tradition, and deep-buried secrets from the past refuse to be hidden forever as the play comes to its shocking climax.

The Whipping Man is a play about redemption and forgiveness, about the lasting scars of slavery, and the responsibility that comes with freedom.

"A mesmerizing drama."
– Peter Filichia, *Newark Star-Ledger*

"A cause for celebration. Mathew Lopez has come as close as any author could to producing a microcosm of the genesis of a wide range of today's Black American males."
– Bob Rendell, *Talkin' Broadway*

SAMUELFRENCH.COM

OTHER TITLES AVAILABLE FROM SAMUEL FRENCH

CREATURE

Heidi Schreck

Dark Comedy / 3m, 3f / Simple Set

After being pestered by devils for more than half a year, Margery Kempe – new mother, mayor's daughter, and proprietress of a highly profitable beer business – is liberated from her torment by a vision of Jesus Christ in purple robes.

Visions are hard to come by, even in 1401. Should we trust the new Margery, with her fasting and her weeping and her chastity fixation, or burn her with the other heretics? Can a woman of insatiable appetites just up an audition for sainthood?

Playwright and OBIE-winning actor Heidi Schreck conjures a collision of contemporary and medieval imaginations: a very funny, a little bit scary new play about faith and its messengers.

"*Creature* indicates that the talented [Heidi Schreck] is a playwright to watch!"
– *New York Post*

"Saints can be hell to live with. That's part of the comedy of *Creature*, Heidi Schreck's absorbing new play about character and faith, loosely based on the life of Margery Kempe, a medieval Englishwoman who, after a difficult childbirth, saw visions of the Devil and Jesus…"
– *The New York Times*

"

SAMUELFRENCH.COM

OTHER TITLES AVAILABLE FROM SAMUEL FRENCH

NEST

Bathsheba Doran

Drama / 5m, 2f

Based on historical fact, *Nest* is a taut domestic love triangle set against the landscape of a fledgling nation on the verge of realizing its manifest destiny at a terrible bloody cost. The play re-imagines the real life story of Susanna Cox, a young indentured servant from Pennsylvania who murdered her baby in 1809, and the story of the man who wrote the ballad that was sold at her hanging. The play is a searing exploration of American dreams and violence and their place in the national psyche.

"[Susanna Cox's] tale is uniquely American, involving all our national obsessions: sexuality, class, gender roles, the search for national identity, and, most of all, the insidious, hypocritical piety coded into our cultural DNA...Doran is particularly deft at constructing dialogue filled with small, characterizing moments to elucidate her themes."
– *Washington City Paper*

"Bathsheba Doran has crafted this seemingly simple but gripping 90-minute work from the true story of Susanna Cox"
– *Talkinbroadway.com*

"*Nest* is no simple costume-drama rendering of [a] young woman's life and death. When the artificial walls of the earlier scenes fall away and the stage is flooded by the cast working as a kind of chorus, one feels the heart of the playwright."
– *MetroWeekly*

SAMUELFRENCH.COM

www.ingramcontent.com/pod-product-compliance
Lightning Source LLC
Chambersburg PA
CBHW070647300426
44111CB00013B/2306